AN ELEPHANT HOLE

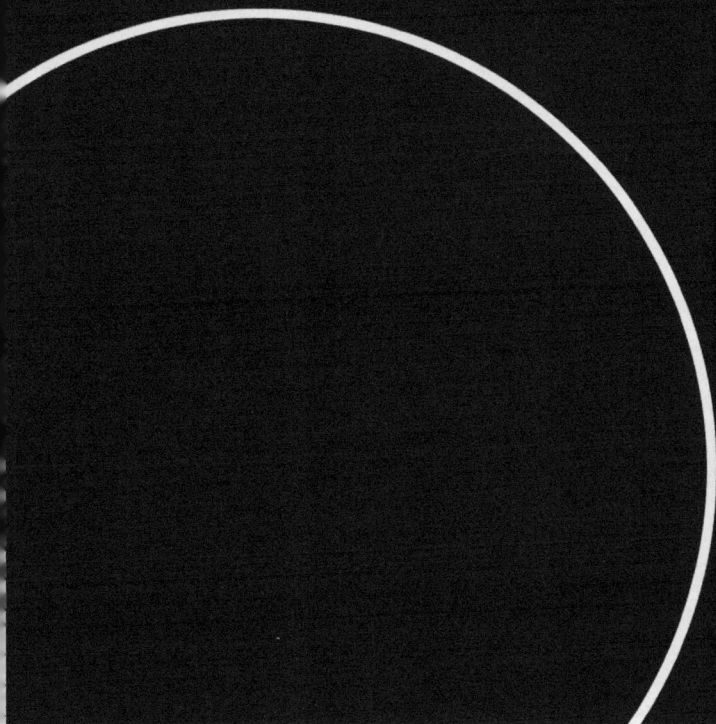

JUSTIN HYDE

AN ELEPHANT HOLE

INTERIOR NOISE PRESS
Austin, Texas

For order information and current mailing address please visit www.interiornoisepress.com

Interior Noise Press
Austin, TX

Book Design by David p Bates

Library of Congress Control Number: 2014931282

ISBN 978-0-9816606-3-9
First Edition

To Ivan.
I can't explain any of this

CON TE N TS

thinking of the cedar river   15
my father is sixty to my twenty-seven   16
got arrested for public intox instead   17
my coworker's hands   19
on the banana boat   21
kid with the broken skateboard   23
i suppose he's earned it   25
ceasar   27
the crux   28
right before the ass-crack of 2am   30
how it mostly went in those days   32
merit badges   33
the man in back who ran the label machine   36
18 days   38
looking at houses   39
i've never bought a roll of toilet paper   43
a poet   44
at the food-court   46
walking down the sidewalk   48
ted kooser   49
polk city iowa   50
a cat's game   51
my relationship with secrets   52
the iron worker   53
at the potato chip warehouse   55
sitting on the grease trap behind taco bell   58
two guys speaking french at the truck stop   60
myriad   62
we all had small lockers
                    in the back of the factory   63
my first poetry reading   64
people   66
reclamation project   67

coffee with vagina 68

in every subway in
    every small midwestern town 72

on that score, i was straight 73

the crackhead 75

the men of eagle iron works 77

at the ronald mcdonald house 78

factory mom 81

bountai 82

sack lunches 84

that man right there 85

edith 87

little park around the block from my house 90

the shipping clerk at ag-leader 92

where do the leaves go? 95

6pm med-line at the work release facility 98

the new fed 99

his checks went for craps
    and blowjobs at the indian casino 101

the man who unlocked my car 102

driving the wedge 104

the torpedo 106

new kid in the snowsuit 107

sitting at the kitchen table of her new
    apartment after closing down the waveland 110

juan 112

mi-mo's funeral 115

an elephant hole 118

a call to the ex wife at 10:27pm 120

raw motherfuckin' business 122

from the book of wtf? 124

my grandfather 126

asking after a coworker 127

wednesday mornings at the waveland 128

write through it 130

sipping a screwdriver at the ghetto bar half mile from my house	131
the first time i met my uncle from tennessee	133
3:38am at the truck stop	135
it's like you don't care about anything	137
if you can believe it	138
cala lilies in the east	140
my trick	141
progression of a body through knives	142
new overnight waitress at the truck stop	144
my grandmother used to read to me	146
wait long enough	149
the trucker's wife	151
turbo	155
how i learned	156
ivan #16	158
childish things	159
only waitress at the truck stop who never uses the cash register	161
my grandfather was a deadeye	163
in iraq	165
grocery shopping for the schizophrenics	166
if we ever meet	167
the qc lady	168
hum in the belly of the spider	169
ten and two	171
down at the alpine tap	174
can you fly emily?	176
in the hallway after taking a piss	177
what i like about you justin	179
the mad scientist	180
at the 24 hour laundry	182
sitting alone at the authentic mexican restaurant	185
there goes the big brazilian	187

at the q on a wednesday
          afternoon in december   189
single mothers, little brown
          assholes like buttons   191
my first time   193
my newest client at work release   196
standing in line to buy lighter fluid and a bic   198
when my father dies   200
for the matriarch   202
the place-mat at the vietnamese restaurant   204
i used to get so very lonely   206
she said i danced like a black man   208
what's the numbers bro?   210
sitting on the curb of the
          square in memphis mo   212
to all the roomates i've
          ever had (newsletter #1)   214
in a low mood   216
i didn't write any poems last night   217
the babysitter   219
ivan can't be alone with grandma   220
sitting in a mcdonald's booth at 2am   221
i'll do it myself daddy   223
a dull lady with big calves   224
why i'm a morning person   226
before we stopped speaking to each other   227
all those faces in high-school   229
dad's underwear   230
when my dad sold the vw rabbit to three asians   231
not all women are cunts   233
watching my father walk out of a gas station   235
fishing with larry   237
when i was eight   238
the only time i remember
          laughing with the old man   240
it ain't all the same   241

at the pool table 243

on being asked about parental influence
          on my creative development as a child 246

god bless america 248

closest the old man and i ever got 250

full circle 251

sixty-three years ago today 252

the last time i saw my father's dad 254

getting your stripes 256

my mother never wore perfume 257

practicing 258

girl on the third shift at the kum and go 259

taking inventory on a hundred
          boxes of rubber grommets 261

you think you've seen everything 263

after falling through the camel's eye 265

it didn't work out 267

in the hospital cafeteria
          while my son has eye surgery 269

at the harvest cafe 271

little church in the basement
          of the county hospital 273

people across the street lost a son in iraq 274

the closest i've come to making love 275

the man watching harness racing at the bar 276

dennis 36 years 278

i've lost the thread 281

arms length 283

this garden, carefully tended, for 32 years 284

no solidarity 285

she told me her mother
          slept with a snub-nosed revolver 286

A hole is nothing at all, but you can break your neck in it.

—Austin O'Malley

thinking of the cedar river

grandpa and i
had our poles in a backwater
waiting on a channel cat
or a blue.

grandpa's friend clarence
was down a ways
trying for smallmouth
in the main river.

clarence got one on

i ran over to watch.

water-opossum,
he spat
unhooking a carp.

goddamned scavenger,
he said
throwing it to the ground
putting the heel of his boot
to its head

same look on his face
my wife had tonight
right before
shoving me into the kitchen counter and
punching me hard in the face

for reasons i've tried deconstructing

but when you get to this point in a marriage
simple cause and effect
slips through the fingers
like this blood
down the drain.

my father is sixty to my twenty-seven

i have come to live in his house again.
when i leave for the factory during the dark of
morning
he sleeps beneath a worn sheet on the couch.

as i tie my boots in the kitchen
dad's naked thigh pales thin,

bony as the skeletons of carp–

quiet on the banks of the des moines river

where we fished.

got arrested for public intox instead

when i was seventeen
dad drove me to a bicycle race
in illinois.

mom must have set it up
because he and i together
was not
normal protocol.

i ended up winning
and there he was
taking pictures.

i'll never forget
his knee high socks
and cutoff jeans
leaning over the curb
with the camera.

six years later
drunk off my ass
at a strip club in davenport
for my best friend's
bachelor party

one of those places
where you bring your own cooler
and fold dollar bills
like tents.

i don't know why
but being there
made me want to call dad
let him know
i remembered that day

how it was important to me.

someone gave me their cell
the bathroom stall didn't have a door
so i huddled in the corner
and started dialing.

then i remembered.

he was supposed to be the one
eventually
making a call like this.

how i was going to hang up on him
when he did.

my coworker's hands

are covered
with blotches of
light pink skin.

she and her boyfriend
were high on meth.
the tv
was still plugged in.
she threw it at him
and it exploded,
burning her hands.

he took off
in her car
with their
three year old boy
saying he was going to
run the both of them
off a bridge.

found the boy
next day
walking in a ditch.

found the car
week later
parked at a rock quarry.
it was all
beaten in
with a bat.

never found
the boyfriend.

her son
is eleven now.
all he remembers

is the
tv exploding.

wish he didn't
have to remember
that much,
she says
and asks again
if i'm sure
about her hands.

she's got
her first date
in years.
guy from huxley
off the internet.

as a man
i promise you
he won't be focused
on your hands,
i tell her.

she smiles.

but you can tell
she doesn't
believe.

on the banana boat

nicodemus
stole a little-debbie truck
from in front of a gas station
while on a whiskey bender.

once you've
crossed a certain line
it's hard to be satisfied
with jesus
and the wisdom of middle managers,
he told me
one night
during a bout of insomnia
at the correctional facility.

he never talked about it
but his file
said he was president of a bank
until his wife
drowned their newborn daughter
and hung herself
from an attic rafter
in ninety-seven.

see you
on the banana boat chief,
is what he said to me
the day
he discharged.

that was
a few
months ago.

this morning
my newspaper tells me
he's been shot to death
trying to break into a

drive through pharmacy
with a sledgehammer.

kid with the broken skateboard

sat next to me
on a downtown bench
and asked
for a dollar.

shouldn't you be
in school?
i asked.

shouldn't you be
at work?
he asked.

he had a green
mohawk

looked to be about
sixteen.

i gave him
the dollar.

he ran
across the street
to walgreens.

the skateboard
in two-pieces
was next to my foot.

i picked up
one of the pieces
spun a yellow wheel.

grinding the science center
stairs,
he said
while sitting back down

and stuffing the last of a snickers
in his mouth.

five-bucks says
i'll clear you,
he said
and picked up the other piece
stood in the middle of the sidewalk
and side-armed it
a good sixty-feet.

double or nothing,
he said
after i cleared him
by three car lengths.

i was clawing back
from thirty-dollars down
when a cop turned the corner
and the kid lit-out
through an alley.

how was work?
my wife asked.

usual bull-shit
and sour bedbugs,
i said.

what's that?
she asked.

i don't know,
i said
and spun
a yellow wheel.

it's important
though.

i suppose he's earned it

withered old man
bearing a striking resemblance
to ted kooser
is pissing next to me
at the truck-stop.

his pants
and underwear
are around
his ankles.

ok
ok
diminished motor skills
he missed the grab
on the way down,
i think to myself.

he passes gas
like a
sick cat

shakes off
in slow motion

then

(baggage claim
still hanging
around his
ankles)

he shuffles
to the sink.

bare pockmarked
white ass
in the reflection

of the glass covering
over the ads
in front of my face

i pinch it off
& get the
hell out of there
before the
third act.

ceasar

at the gym five in the morning on my days off
i started noticing this
raw boned hispanic on the treadmill
not much in the way of an anomaly
until you notice he's running in steel toed boots
and cut-off jeans
hauling ass too
bet he pegs it eight or nine miles an hour.
between sets of pull ups
i passed him stepping off the thing
asked if he was
training for a five k or something.
in broken english i caught
he runs four miles
seven days a week.
his father recently died of a heart attack
doctors say he's got risk
doesn't want to leave his wife
and three kids without a provider.
he's about my size
was gonna offer him a pair of old running shoes
but he had to cut out for work.
pours concrete with a dewitt crew: a known employer of illegals.
watching him head off
i think

these are the people stealing our jobs?
i say lets pay em a fair wage.
i'll take this guy as a countryman
over any batch of bloated entitlement
you'd snag out of a union hall
with a gar hook
these days.

the crux

there's a certain
feral
part of me
i'm not willing
to kill off,
i say
to the
marriage counselor.

he just needs
to fucking
grow up,
my wife says
cold-blooded
arms folded
vice-tight
against her
chest.

he scratches
his widows peak.

my job
is to help you
understand each other
not so much
give advice,
he said
at our
first session.

he's all arms and legs
underfed stork
with a mouth-full
of bleached
teeth.

i like
the guy,
i think to myself
lunging towards him
with a series of
low-bellied barks
from the spine.

he falls off
his chair.

i start laughing
uncontrollably.

everything's one big
goddamn joke,
she says
followed by the chessboard
off the coffee table
three times hard
into the
side of my face.

right before the ass-crack of 2am

i remembered
to grab a
couple forties.

kid
at the truck stop register
was sitting on a stool
hunched over his cell phone.

i waited
quite a while before
lightly clanking
the forties together.

oh shit man
hope you haven't been
standing there long,
he said
hopping off the stool.

not long at all,
i said.

dude
i'm sorry
i can't sell you that
it's past two.

i pointed to the
clock on the wall
it said:
1:53am.

oh damn
sorry man
never should have put
guitar hero
on my cell phone

it's got me all spaced out,
he said
ringing me up.

no problem
happens to the best of us,
i said
tossed the forties in my car
and went back to the trucker's lounge
where i was reading plato's account
of socrates' death.

he was ordered
to drink hemlock
for corrupting
the minds of
athenian youth.

imagine if socrates
showed up in america
today:

he'd probably walk coast to coast
couple times
until he realized
what he was working with.

then he'd disappear
quietly into the woods
and send sparrows skyward
unzipping his soul
with a .357

how it mostly went in those days

unpacking my stuff
first day of college
i found some
4x8 photos
in the bottom
of a box.

head-shots
from kindergarten
through seventh grade.

i'm not sure why
i taped them
in a vertical line
on the back
of my dorm door.

what's that
all about?
my roomate asked
when he moved in
the next week.

there's something
between those pictures,
i told him.
an unseen force
pulling all of us
unwillingly.

he didn't
say anything
right then.

but two days later
he moved out.

merit badges

little before five on a tuesday

i work third shift

should be asleep
on that mattress over there
corner of the basement

but i'm on the couch
in the dark
working through a
tepid case of
bud light
trying to decide
if i should laugh or cry
over the last decade.

door opens

lights flicked on

my son
month shy of
two years old
comes plodding in.

wife goes upstairs

we don't talk much these days

this is how she says

time to get up.

tuesday nights
she watches tv
at a friend's house

i hear the front door close

car start.

what doin' daddy?
he asks
sing-song voice
picking up a can
off the floor.

what this?
he hands it to me.

he's never seen me
drinking

drunk a few times

but i had this
pollyanna notion
i'd be able to
hide it from him.

these are daddy's merit badges,
i say.

merit badges,
he parrots
disturbingly
clear.

ivan do?
he asks
as i finish off the one
in my hand.

not until you're twelve,
i smile

pick him up

playfully bite his neck

spear two hot dogs with a fork

and hold them over the stove

for dinner.

the man in back who ran the label machine

dave was having problems
with his kid:
twenty-three years old
running through jobs
two owi's.

you can't talk to him
thinks he wrote the book,
dave told me once
at lunch break.

the janitor paul
told me
it was dave's own making.
said the kid
came to live with dave
when he was
four years old
after his mother died.
said dave told him
how the kid
would try to snuggle with him
on the couch
but dave would
push him away.

when a kid wants to snuggle
you don't push em away
you open your arms

wide as you can
then wider still,
paul said
eyes twisted
with hurt.

paul had a
fifth grade education.

he used the word nigger
and had a payee
to keep track of his money.

but sometimes
he made more sense
than the rest of us.

18 days

says the
second shift supervisor
as i pass him
in the parking lot
on the way in.

they're
euthanizing him
after forty-seven years
of service.

what-cha
gonna do with yourself?
i ask.

says
he's got
projects around home
to last
until spring:

then fuck
i don't know

maybe i'll get a dog
or some of that viagra.

says he
hasn't gone at marcine
with the old shoe-horn
since before mash
went off
air.

looking at houses

as we pulled a right off university
i saw a human figure
face down
on a basketball court
behind the grade school.

hey turn into the school
looks like
somebody might be hurt,
i said to my wife.

probably just
some drunk
homeless person,
she said
and kept going.

no seriously
go back there,
i said.

no seriously
we're not
going back there,
she said
sarcastically.

i looked at her
for a second.

then i grabbed the steering wheel
and said
let me out of the fucking car.

she stopped.
i got out.
she kept going.

it was a young
black kid.

hey
you alright man?
i asked.

he looked up.
his eyes were
red with tears.

i'll be alright,
he said.

i saw you from the road
just wanted to make sure
you were ok,
i said.

thanks,
he said
and dropped his head
back into his arms.

i stood on the corner

a good five minutes
before my wife pulled up.

so?
she asked coldly.

i don't know
some young black kid
problems at home
or something.

we drove in silence
then she said:

you could have been killed
it could have been
some crazy person
then what?
you leave your wife
and son
with no husband
or father.

i told her:
you have no heart.
you're what's wrong with
the world.
you have no compassion.

she didn't say anything
but her knuckles
got tighter
on the
steering wheel.

i told her:
what if that had been
our son
wouldn't you want someone to stop?
don't we owe that
to each other as a species
at the bare minimum?

get out! get out! get out
of the fucking car!
she screamed.

i got out
amidst heavy traffic
on university avenue.

it was a good
nine miles

back to our apartment.

i walked back
to the basketball court.

the kid was gone.

i sat down
where he had been.

i've never bought a roll of toilet paper

or a bed
or owned a hundred dollar pair of shoes
or voted for anything
or missed a meal
or seen the ocean
or lived anywhere besides iowa
but last night at the truck-stop
this full blooded cherokee
off a reservation in arkansas
said he was hitching to vegas for a nine-ball tournament
been four days since he'd seen water
lived by a lake back home
bruising his spirits not to see any water
i drove him to the pond behind bird-land park
there in the moonlight
he stripped naked
tossed his britches on the hood of my car
and uncorked a swan-dive
out of a dead sprint
off the end
of the floating dock.

a poet

is not
an actual human being.

he is a grotesque
anchored
at the periphery.

he only exists
to watch and analyze
actual human beings.

he knows this

carries it around inside him
like a graveyard
sitting at PD's pub
seven in the morning
with a handful of women
off third shift
from the firestone plant.

they're laughing like hyenas
telling a story
about the retarded janitor
who got down on one knee
in the break-room
and proposed to the hr manager
with a
hundred dollar ring from wal-mart.

he laughs along with them
but only because he knows
he should be laughing.

his body is amongst them
but his mind stands at a distance
cataloguing it all.

their laughter is perfect
like blue velvets
like a bowl of cold cherries
or a symphony.

he envies
their laughter.

their lives
in perfect motion
without thought.

at the food-court

teenage cottontails
hop on by

you imagine
pinning them down
pumping lightning
splitting their sides
up the seams.

your wife
folds her
napkin

her face
makes you
sick

you think
she's weak
and needy

you're
wrong.

that dark haired
father of two
behind you

right now
she's imagining
his breath
across the hairs
of her neck

the rough brush
of his hand
down the length

of her
thigh

she's got
three different ways
in mind
to get rid of you
with no evidence

but she'd also
kill a man
and bury him
for you.

she's a
ten millimeter
locked and loaded
with hollow points

and you don't even
know it.

walking down the sidewalk

a car
pulled into the driveway
of a duplex
up ahead.

a large
old
bosnian lady
bobbed down the driveway
picked her little granddaughter
out of the backseat
held her up
in her arms
spinning her around.

we smiled
at each other
as i passed by.

it felt good

that simple
human
warmth.

like i might
float up
into the sky.

like we wouldn't
fight to the death
as soon as
food and water
became scarce.

ted kooser

started
showing up
in my sunday
newspaper.

he chooses a poem
from the abyss
and writes an
introduction.

i've read each one
four weeks running.

it's helped me
better understand
the readers and editors
of the poetry magazines
i don't bother
submitting to:

poetry is something
they do
after the bills are paid
eaves are cleaned out
the hedges are equidistant
all properties
and vehicles
insured.

these are good citizens
they vote in school board elections
replace break-lights the day
they go out.

only then
come their poems
jogging along
in l.l. bean fleece.

polk city iowa

as you rack a game of nine ball
in the tavern
and sip a draw of coors

the noon bell goes off
in this small town
you only drove to
because the realtor
set up an open house
and your presence
on a twin bed mattress
in the basement
of an otherwise empty home
would be a detriment
to this final step
in the separation
of your family.

you finish the beer
tuck the cue flush with the bumper
staring disinterestedly
at a fishing show
on the tv.

then you walk outside
and sit on a bench
next to an empty fountain
in the middle of the town square.

it starts raining.

a cold rain
down your arms
like glass.

a cat's game

my coworker has a private relationship with jesus
for which i consider him
an intellectual stillbirth.
i get drunk five days a week
have anonymous sex
with women i meet in bars
and walk around like socrates
peeling back layers of whale-fat and jello
searching for coherence amongst asbestos and flightless birds
for which he pities my eternal soul.
last night i told him it's a cat's game.
how we're both getting hustled
by a cistern
in all of us.

my relationship with secrets

i was thirteen the day i found a half-full bottle of vodka behind the
chainsaw blade sharpener in my grandfather's small engine repair shop.
by then i was no stranger to secrets, having already discovered the letters
in mom's underwear drawer from her college friend in postville.
for the kids, she agreed with mom, best to stay together for the kids;
we can't be selfish in these things.
my father didn't hide his drinking, but he kept photographs
in a small rusted tackle-box beneath the wheel-jack in the trunk of his car.
him and a beautiful brown skinned woman from when he was stationed in
the philippines.
they were hugging or kissing in most of them;
it was the only evidence that my dad had ever smiled.
some nights i'd go out the front door,
sneak into the neighbors backyard to where i could see him through the
side window, locked in the garage with his liquor and tackle-box flipped
open in his lap.
knowing grown-ups had secrets made me feel better about how i hadn't
said anything that whole summer. sitting alone in the basement, i'd been
thinking over and over about riding my bicycle in front of one of those
red dump trucks that ran back and forth
in front of our house
to and from the rock quarry.

the iron worker

leaning against his truck
smoking a cigarette
waiting on material
for the new office space
one building over

as two stories above
i drink coffee
mixed with crown
and work my way
through schopenhauer's
madness.

the secret of blue collar work
few realize
and even fewer appreciate
is that your body might be
subjugated to machine
but you get to keep your
mind:

your hands might be
torquing a four-headed cap press
but upstairs
you're trying to figure
how in the hell karl marx
got socialism
from hegel

or

you might be on a hog farm
sitting backwards on a sow
draining a packet of boar-semen into her cunt
while trying to
wrap your mind around
a-priori knowledge.

i learned the hard way
white collar work
is nothing but
whoring out your mind
to insipidly pedantic
crossword puzzles

which

if you have more
than a lemming-compass
and base-ten blueprints
for a mind
is the equivalent
of daily bone-grafts
without anesthesia.

problem is
most of these blue collar guys
don't take advantage:

they work logic
and tiddlywink polemics
off a handful of
crackhead premises

most of them
glass-eyed shriners
turning lifetimes
of zero-g figure eights.

this guy's cellphone
hanging from a
dale junior lanyard
and the set of
bright orange plastic testicles
dangling from the back bumper of his truck
tell me all i need to know
about which slope of the bell curve
he's nailed to.

at the potato chip warehouse

they don't stack pallets
flush with the wall.

there's a foot-wide line
painted white
all around
the perimeter.

it's called the rat run.

i was the chump temp
brought in
to repaint it.

before i could repaint it
i had to
sweep up the rat shit.

all gotta make bank somehow,
said the black forklift driver
nodding down at me
with my broom and
buckets of paint.

paper-paper money,
i smiled
feeling pretty good
(i come from a long line of faulty-wires
who get satisfaction
from physical labor).

it was all lateral motion

my shoulders were too wide to
turn
between the wall
and stacks of pallets.

broke a good sweat

got a rhythm

then the first bump on my foot

then the next.

kept coming
every couple minutes.

only light back there
was zebra stripes
through the pallet slats.

stood still for awhile
watching brown lumps
shoot the gaps

then i left the mop
moon-walked out the back
and jumped off
the loading dock.

hey,
forklift driver
called after me.

you lasted longer
than the other three,
he smiled.

thanks,
i smiled
and flashed him
peace.

i hopped on my bicycle wondering
where i was going to

sleep that night.

warehouse manager came out hotbox
hands waving
over his head.

meep-meep,
i said
and coasted past him

merging
onto the paved shoulder
of a
very busy highway.

sitting on the grease trap behind taco bell

i was supposed to be
on a greyhound
bound for a fishing boat
in alaska

but i'd
walked past the station
and tossed my ticket
over the fence
of the
catholic school playground.

i was twenty six

living in my parent's basement
after imploding as a bank examiner
for the federal reserve

all my possessions
were in the hiking pack
to my left.

even as a young kid
in the trailer park
faking sick from school
for a little solitude

i knew
it was going to end
like this.

sitting there
on that grease trap
hum of tire
up and down lincoln way
i was surprised
i'd held things together
long as i did.

my old boss
from the bicycle shop
pretended not to see me
as he walked past
to his car.

serendipity,
i thought to myself

and laid back

and

closed my eyes.

two guys speaking french at the truck stop

feels
like i'm at some
paris cafe
out of the
diaries of anais nin
instead of the flying j
in des moines iowa.

i have
no clue
what they're
talking about

but it's got
mellifluous cadence

warm wax
through deep center
like the wave machine
my last girlfriend
kept in her bedroom.

i could easily
spend the rest of my life
slung low
in a sidewalk cafe
smoking opium laced cigarettes

listening to this language
as the sun
sank below
the arc de triomphe.

but the clock says
10:34pm

my child support payment
of 527.91

is due by
noon tomorrow

and my shift
locked in a pit
with the murderers
rapists
and other failed
hustlers of iowa

starts
in exactly
26 minutes.

myriad

the hiring manager
at UPS
had never seen anyone
use

- myriad -

in a job application.

as in:

- i have myriad skills applicable to this job -

i've got more qualified apps
but i like your enthusiasm,
were his exact words.

i was seventeen years old
that day

ten years before i'd read
or write
my first poem.

more proof that poets

are born

full of shit.

we all had small lockers in the back of the factory

tom had two polaroids
taped to the back
of his door.

his girls

twelve and
seven.

he went to sarah's
softball practice
every wednesday
and saturday.

he said
if they happened
to be in a public place
at the same time

it was ok
that they
walked out to his lawn chair
and gave him a hug.

but his wife
up there in the stands
with her boyfriend
and that phony
restraining order.

the bitch
wouldn't let
little jenny
come down.

my first poetry reading

a meek
well groomed man
no taller
than a barber's chair
stood in back
smiling like a serial killer
the whole time.

afterward
he bought
my book

asked me to
sign it.

i asked
how he'd heard
of the reading.

oh
in the newspaper,
he said shyly
voice like fish oil
dripping onto
tin-foil.

the ted bundy smile
was still plastered
on his face:

i swear i
saw a monkey-paw
in the back-pocket
of his jeans

but he quickly
reached around

pushing whatever it was
back down.

you're probably
more interesting
than the people
i'm about to
have drinks with,
i wrote
in the
book-jacket

shook his hand

&

told him:

never lose that smile.

it splits atoms.

people

one on one
they'll acknowledge
the ambiguity
of this whole catastrophe

own up to fears

and the irrationality
of their biases.

get a group though
and the ego

insecurities

and chickenshit blood
start dribbling
down their chins.

it's the worst goddamn b flick
you've ever seen

only there you are
smack-fuck
in the middle.

reclamation project

take the drunk
from the bottle

he is left
with the heavy machinery
of his mind
hanging from a rope
like a busted tractor engine
in a barn.

he stands
at a distance

eying
the strange contraption
skeptically.

sunlight

coming through the windows
for the first time in years

frightens him
immensely.

coffee with vagina

first
i noticed her glasses:
black square rims.
abnormal camouflage
maybe she's got something,
i thought to myself.

then
i noticed her ass:
bubble butt,
a real apple-bottom.
i'm a lush for
that kind of eclipse.

i sat there at the bar
alternating shots of black velvet
and bottles of bud light
trying to forge
an angle.

she seemed like the
kind of girl
who'd read ayn rand,
the kind of girl
who'd appreciate
an original
off-speed pitch.

finally decided
i'd tell her
she had the
physiognomy
of an eccentric.

she walked by
to the restroom
while i was playing pool

with a city snowplow driver
named frank.

when she came out
i asked
if i could tell her something.

go,
she said.

you've got the
physiognomy
of an eccentric,
i told her.

how long did it
take for you to
come up
with that?

off the cuff
purely off the cuff,
i told her.

what else you got?
she asked.

there's something solemn
in your face
that outlasts the crowd,
i told her.

that's just
more of the same,
she said
and went back
to a table full of
fleece and wool:

carbon credits
and patronizers of
urban
farmers markets.

what was that
all about chief?
asked frank.

i gave her
my best knuckle ball
but she didn't flinch,
i said
and chalked my cue.

i think she takes her
coffee with vagina
if you know
what i mean,
he said.

that's good
ego salve,
i said.

nice ass though,
he said.

like a
snowplow,
i said.

ha ha
that made
him laugh.

i sipped my
crown and seven

scanning
the horizon
for something more
amiable.

in every subway in every small midwestern town

there is a middle aged woman
face of clay
butcher's forearms

a single dry leaf
dangling in the wind
behind her eyes.

you don't make small-talk
about the weather.

you don't say anything
about the onions
you didn't ask for.

you just get your change

and leave.

ashamed to have
intruded
on her
sarcophagus.

on that score, i was straight

i spent lunch breaks
at the ryko factory
on a rusted I-beam
out back.

a cornfield
ran right up to the edge
of the gravel road
semis used
to deliver iron
and stainless.

across the cornfield
was a highway—

in those cars
were people with
loaded dice
and no hands.

beyond that
i didn't have
a clue.

sometimes
i'd come close
to some semblance
of an answer

but right about then
the plant's electronic 'gong'
pierced through
my earplugs
into my spine.

the big japanese lazer
was hungry for the
hundred pound sheets of stainless

i spent ten hours a day
sweating through five shirts
loading onto it.

and if i didn't want to feed it
they'd get some other loser
with limited options
from the temp agency
within the hour.

the crackhead

tells me
he and his father
caught chubs
out of a creek
behind the airport
but he never could put a worm
on the hook
cause he'd imagine himself
as the worm
how much
it must have hurt.
says
there was a pregnant
street-woman
at the bus stop today
he heard her
talking to a friend
she was craving ice cream
he bought her a drumstick
from the walgreens
across the street
she started crying.
his hands shake constantly
he pushes his finger
into his head
above his left eye
says he can feel another migraine
coming on.
mr. justin
(that's what he calls me,
i'm his parole officer)
you done told me
you was an atheist
somethin awful
must have happened
for you to think that way—
i don't expect you'll tell me what

but i'll help you see
yet,
he smiles
showing a top row of empty teeth
and holds out
his hand.

the men of eagle iron works

smudged black
head to toe
smoking cigarettes
while leaning against pickups
in the back parking lot
during morning break

give me strange brow
as i cruise by
on the bicycle path
clad in spandex.

they probably
think i'm
independently wealthy

or have some other
white collar hustle

to be
dressed like a queer
riding my bicycle
at ten a.m.
on a tuesday.

but i'm
hung over
like a
dead moose

myself
having to
punch the clock
two hours from now
at the ryko factory
for a
mandatory ten.

at the ronald mcdonald house

i always thought this place
was for poor people,
but the hospital recommended
we stay here
the night before
my son's eye surgery.

he and my ex-wife
are already asleep
up in the room.

i'm sitting on a couch
in a little lounge
full of stuffed animals and books
trying to decide
if i should go find a bar
or get some sleep.

two little black kids
are playing with crayons
in the corner.

the older one
with his arm in a sling
grabs a book off the shelf.
he walks over
and asks
if i'll read it to him.

(he looks old enough
to be able to read)

i ask him to
read it
to me.

i can't read,
he says

chewing on his finger
while looking down
at the floor.

he sits to my left.
his little sister
sits to my right.
i read them a book
about a dog
who runs away from home
because he's afraid
of baths.

we read it
over and over.
they ask a million questions.
it's like nobody ever
read them a book before.

devon!
tanisha!
you leave that man be,
says a large woman
standing in the doorway
of the lounge.

she looks drunk

or high.

no
they're alright
i was just reading them
a couple
books.

suit yourself,
she says

disappearing
down the hall.

we huddle back in
and read
where the wild things are
for the
seventh time
in a row.

factory mom

i don't wanna be a factory mom,
joni said
half-hour
into a mandatory twelve.

she was four months along
just starting to show.

wanna get a secretary job
something in an office
away from all these fucking chemicals

but my typing isn't very good,
she said
as we taped up another box
of swimming pool ph strips.

told her
she could take some typing classes at night.

said
she probably couldn't afford that.

told her
they probably offered them free
at the community center.

sounds like alot of work,
she said
pulling off her favre jersey
grabbing the marlboro's
out of her locker
as first break buzzer
cut cadence
over the speakers.

bountai

was the janitor
at my
elementary
school.

he'd give us
cookies
from the cafeteria
if we helped
sweep the steps
during recess.

i always
helped him
carry the brooms
back to
the storage area
behind a small door
in the gym
wall.

it reeked
of bleach
and window
caulk.

he had
a rusty folding chair
stuffed in the corner
a little
shower radio
and a
warped
black and white photo
of flat faced
stoic people
that looked
like him.

if he told me
why his wife and kids
were still
back in vietnam
i don't remember.

all i recall
for sure
is that principal mcdermat
caught him
drinking from a flask
up on the roof
and i never saw him
again.

sack lunches

at the work release center
consist of
government grade meat and cheese
a small sack of plain lays
and a packet of
instant
sugarless
grape koolaid. i'm only
supposed to give them one each
when they leave for work
but i hide an extra
behind the smoke shack
for tuttle
when i do my midnight grounds check
because i found out
he was giving his away
to an underfed husky
he came across
cutting through the old save u more lot
on the way to dee-zee
where he screws handles
on screen doors. the world
don't give a shit
for either of us
so he and i
we gotta watch out
for each other,
he told me
this morning
as i buzzed him out
the security door.

that man right there

pouring concrete
for a kentucky fried chicken
on southeast 14th
did eighteen years
maximum security in
pelican bay for
running meth with the
hells angels and stabbing
a cop.

he's at work release for
one year then
ten years on
federal parole.

i've personally
seen him do sixteen
one-armed pull-ups
if he said 'boo' the
piss in your bladder
would freeze.

yesterday
three in the morning
i was sitting next to him
in the chow hall
while he bawled.

it was the fifth anniversary
of his
mother's death
which he wasn't allowed to
attend
while in federal prison.

sometimes the
heartache's enough to
choke out any light,

he said before
composing himself.

one more and i'll
get out of your hair
boss?
he asked
pulling a marlboro
from behind his ear.

they aren't supposed to smoke
after eleven at night
but i gave him
the go ahead.

us short guys gotta
stick together,
he smiled
after lighting up and
showed me how to
take out a knee
permanently
with my shoulder in a
split second
just in case
one of these fuck-nut cons
ever decided to get
froggy with me.

edith

she had ankles
like telephone poles

butcher's forearms

whale gut

stench of formaldehyde
from beneath a
billowing
denim skirt.

i couldn't decide if she was retarded
or just a little slow.
we were cleaning
a street full
of college apartments
between summer
and fall lease.

they randomly assigned us in tandems
paid us by the apartment

i thought she'd be a liability
but she worked like a clydesdale.

right then
we'd been at it
thirty-six hours straight.

she leaned against a sycamore
picking a scab on her forearm
and i sat on the front steps
while the apartment manager
checked our work.

she'd go hours without saying anything
then she'd ask my favorite color

if i'd ever kissed a girl
what kind of cake i liked on my birthday.

i'd gathered
she lived with her dad
out in the country
near gilbert

she liked giraffes
her favorite color
was green.

she pulled her sleeve down
wiped blood from the scab
then she asked
if i wanted to get married.

just like that.

told her
i wouldn't make
a very good husband.

she told me
her dad said
she was rotten fruit

that she'd never find a husband.

i told her
that wasn't true

that she'd make a beautiful wife.

her face went red.

the apartment manager came down
flashed thumbs up

said head over to that complex
across the street.

.

little park around the block from my house

cute kid,
a woman on the bench
calls to me
as i wipe wind-tears
pooling at the bottom
of his eyes.

diana is loose at the edges
but i've always liked
a little extra
within reason.

her daughter
climbs the jungle gym
as i bounce my son
on my knee.

we turn in on each other
share easy laughs
about these creatures
who've upended our lives
like atomic bombs
we don't regret.

she keeps tucking
small strands of blond hair
behind her ears

kicking
of her right foot
brushes softly
against my ankle.

a man gets
to a certain
age.

he can read the heat

from a woman
like an oil-dipstick.

or all the unnamed
hurricanes

welling up
inside him.

the shipping clerk at ag-leader

put out more
than thirty cigarettes
into the top of his
right hand.

did it in
his early
twenties:

he'd flunked out of
iowa state

was bouncing at
a strip club &
selling e.

said he
hated himself back then
but didn't have the guts
for suicide.

now
he was convinced
he'd never get a real job
because of the scar.

said his family
ran an asian grocery store
down in florida:

missed the hell out of them

probably get a good job there

but he was a nothing.

too ashamed to call

let alone visit.

i only got him
to come drinking
once.

after a couple
shots of tequila he
got real serious.

told me he
wasn't worth
loving.

then he
pulled me in close

asked if i'd
put a bullet
in his head.

said he had a
revolver
back in his
apartment.

i told him no

he tried playing it off
like a joke:

ordered us shots of
151

bummed a smoke off
the bartender calm
as a sunday dress he
lit it up

pulled a mammoth drag.

then he buried it
into the top of
his left hand.

where do the leaves go?

sitting on the curb
outside the laundry mat
on army post

hung-over
to the point of
peripheral flashes of light.

one of the little cholos
came out
asked me for a dollar.

i'd already
told him no
four or five times.

how do you say
go sew your mouth shut
in spanish?
i asked jokingly
because for a little shit
he had personality.

it was windy that day

an ocean of leaves
blew through the parking lot.

what happens to the leaves?
he asked
while twisting a valve cap
off a pickup.

they vacation
in tijuana
for the winter,
i said
rubbing my temples.

no
for serious
where do they go?
he asked
writing something in spanish
into the dust
on the side of the truck
with his finger.

the ground
eats them,
i said.

for serious?

for serious.

will the ground
eat me?
he asked.

someday
if you're lucky,
i said.

mama says
we go to heaven,
he said
looking up through the laundry mat window
at clay faced mama
catatonic in a plastic chair

his five brothers and sisters
dirty shrews
darting around her feet.

your mom has to believe that
otherwise she'd drown you
and your brothers and sisters

and burn your father alive,
i wanted to say.

but what i said was:

mama favors mysticism
over syllogism
but she might well
be right.

then i reached down
into my sock
pulled out a five

told him run across the street
get me some tylenol
and he could
keep the change.

6pm med-line at the work release facility

mr. jarvis takes liver pills,
heart pills,
gout pills, schizophrenia pills
and insulin shots.
he's a sixty-two years old
burned out
needle freak
barely making it
through each workday
at the tennis-shoe recycling plant.
he's shown me pictures in his room
he was a green beret
in vietnam,
the 72 gto
he flipped in the ditch
killing his first wife.
i check under his tongue
after each pill,
initial beside his initial in the med-log.
i have this idea justin,
i could take an ad out in the paper
people could call me up
when they get lonely
or just feeling low,
i could meet them for coffee.
i'd call it phone-a-friend,
you think
i could do some good
that way?

the new fed

young kid
maybe twenty-three

eyes like van gogh

more soul than normal
for these parts.

spent thirty-four hours
on a greyhound
coming to work release
from federal prison
in kentucky.

have to sit next to any crazies?
i ask
while checking in the contents
of his green army bag.

matter of fact no,
he says

tells me he sat next to a
young woman
and her six year old daughter.

it was nice,
he says

tells me
he felt human
for the first time
in five years.

says the little girl
got attached to him
pretty quick

he bought her
a package of super-balls
during a two-hour layover
in indiana

the three of them
started bouncing them around
having so much fun
they almost missed the bus.

they get off in des moines too?
i ask
handing him some intake forms
to sign.

no

no,
he says

tells me
they had to go on to omaha.

maybe next time,
i say
pointing out his room
down the hall.

such is life,
he says
and shoulders his bag
and asks
which way to the can.

his checks went for craps and blowjobs at the indian casino

if i had your accent
i'd probably own my own factory,
henry told me at lunch break
in his clipped
vietnamese.

i told him:

look henry
your english isn't half bad
on top of that
you're an intelligent guy
if i were you
i'd put in
for that third shift
supervisor position.

no
no,
he waved me off
lit another cigarette
and reached his hand
under the picnic table.

he came up with a leaf.

this is all i'm meant for,
he said

lighting it on fire.

the man who unlocked my car

that'll be
eighty dollars,
he said
after thirty seconds
with a
long-wire tool.
seventy if you pay cash.

all i got's
a check,
i said.

don't take checks.
cash or credit.

i knocked
on the front door.
christ! always something with you,
she said
disappearing
into the house
to get her credit card.

my ex-wife,
i said.
accidentally
locked my keys
in the car
and blocked her in
dropping off my son.
she's got a date
or something.

i got a couple
ex-wives,
he said
and pulled up his shirt
showing an oblong scar

above his belly-button.
coat-hanger
at close-range,
he smiled.

thank you mam,
he said
and took the card
and tipped his chiefs hat
showing a
crater-like indentation
left of
his widow's peak.

twenty-two pistol
from across the living room,
he said
tapping the crater
before i had
a chance to ask.

i liked him,
i said to my ex
as he
pulled
out of the drive.

why don't you go
write one of your
precious poems about him,
she said
slamming the door
in my face.

driving the wedge

derrick would rather be
hit by a truck
than hurt anyone's feelings
but colton says whatever
pops into his mind,
says the guy
drinking next to me
at southport.

tells me
his ex-wife
has a boyfriend
living with her
and his two boys.

says his boys
never talk about the guy
when he has them
on weekends

how the older boy
might be protecting his feelings
but the younger boy
blabs about everything.

doesn't make any sense
you'd think
they'd have something to say
about the guy
one way
or the other,
he says
finishing off
his beer.

i ask my ex
about him

but she says
none of my business–

she just keeps
driving the wedge,
he says
spinning the empty glass
like a top
and pretending
to laugh.

the torpedo

you bunch up
even if you're not in a gang
for protection i mean
you held? a cholo asked
during pill line
my first day in gen-pop
i didn't know what the hell he was getting at
said i could be a torpedo for the ms-13
or get my ass run through
bruised ribs on a daily basis
i was in there a year
before they called my number
some guy
older than my grandpa
sex offender i guess
making eyes on someone's kids during visitation
at chow andale
they told me out on the yard
slipped a padlock into my hand
look at me
i'm a weed dealer not some hard-ass
never been in a fight my whole life
ruptured his eardrum
made the poor fucker
blind in the right eye
it was him or me.

new kid in the snowsuit

said his name
was chad
and sat down
next to me
on the steps
at recess.

he was
in sixth grade.
i was
in fourth.

middle of june.
i didn't know why
he wore a snowsuit
every day.
didn't ask,
didn't care,
it was nice to
have someone
to talk to.

told me
his dad
fought in vietnam.

i lied
told him
my dad
had been in
vietnam too.

we decided
they must have been
in the
same platoon.

he was going to

ask his dad about it
when he came back from utah
which he said
should be any day now.

sitting on the stairs
we played a game
seeing how close
we could toss pebbles
to a patch of grass
growing out of the
cracked playground.

the pebbles were grenades
and the patch of grass
was a gook hut.

while we played
we joked about how many
chink gooks
we were going to rape.

he'd say
he was going to
rape six of em
in the throat.

then i'd say
i was going to
rape ten of em
in the eyes.

it went on
like that
for a couple weeks.
until a woman
and a man in a suit
took him away from school

in the
middle of the day.

i heard a teacher
say something about
foster care.

some of the
kids said
he'd
murdered someone.

i didn't know
exactly where
they took him.

but out there
at recess

i was
alone on the steps
again.

**sitting at the kitchen table of her new apartment
after closing down the waveland**

she tells me
he mowed over
the rose bushes
she planted
four years ago
shortly after
they were married.

out of spite
because she wouldn't
change the
visitation schedule
for their
three year old son.

so cold
on a dime,
she says
trying to snap
her fingers
but making
no sound.

the person
you love
turning on you
like that

can you
even imagine
the person you love
turning on you
like that?

before
i can answer

she starts
crying.

this low moan
from the gut

standing
every hair
along my neck
on end.

juan

is the new foreman
at the screen-door factory
where six guys
from work-release
are on
second shift.

they're due back at eleven
but juan usually
calls twice a night
extending them to
four or five
in the morning.

cluster-fuck down there,
the guys say
coming back completely spent
hands blistered up
like crabs.

they're always
three weeks
behind on orders
missing this part
that part:

the guys get
seventy plus hours a week
if they want it.

new foreman
sounds like a decent guy,
i tell them.

they tell me
juan's better than
the guy that just got fired

how that bastard
stayed in his office
playing computer solitaire

but juan's
out on the floor
working just as hard as
any of them.

polish check forger
tells me
juan gets by
on two hours sleep:

how he drops
the six of them off
at work-release
goes home
and sleeps
from seven to nine

then watches
his five kids
while his wife
goes to work.

insanity,
we all agree.

tonight
a guy named jake
called into work-release
to extend the guys.

what happened to juan?
i ask
when they get back.

hadn't it

made the news?
they ask.

as i pat them down
and run the metal detector
they tell me how
juan lost his marbles:

he'd fired a pistol
into the ceiling of his house
beat his wife
with the butt end of the thing
lit her car on fire
and disappeared
into the woods.

nobody says a word.

we just nod silently there

knowing full well
juan could be
any one of us.

mi-mo's funeral

the young man
ran broadside
into my passenger door
as i sat stopped
at the intersection
of fifty-seventh
and merle hay.

he picked himself
up
and kept going.

the heel
of his left foot
wasn't touching
the ground
and his torso
seemed to be fighting
his legs.

i pulled
alongside him
rolled down my window
and asked
if he was ok.

bas bas
i mis du bas,
he shouted urgently
without stopping.

his fingers were splayed
and twisted
and his left arm
was folded up tight
near his collarbone.

you need a ride?

he was sweating profusely
at the forehead
snot running heavy
from both nostrils.

where you headed?

he was so worked up
he couldn't get it out.
all he could muster
were grunts
while pointing left
or right
with his good hand.

we came upon the church
as the funeral procession
was snaking
out of the parking lot.

mi-mo! mi-mo!
he shouted
and clawed furiously
at the door.

hey, i'll take you,
don't worry,
i'll get you there,
just calm down.

an old man
in a cadillac
waved us
into the line.

we got stopped
at a train crossing
and before i could grab him

he flung the door open
and took off.

dropped to his knees
and threw his arms
around the back
of the hearse.

an elephant hole

chuck
was the trailer-park manager:

dark-blue
one-piece
mechanic's suit

ash-white buzz-cut

liver-rorschach
up and down his arms.

yelled in my face
when i was seven

accused me of digging
an elephant hole
in the sand
below the jungle-gym.

made us
use a cat-ball
when we played baseball.

wouldn't let us
roam around
with sticks
and hammers:

basically
an epic
cock-block.

we gave good repechage though:

poured orange-juice
into the community lawn-mowers
he had to service

took dumps
on the floor of the party room
below the laundry-mat

cut tags
off gas meters

and

constantly wrote:
'die fat whore'

on the windshield of his wife's k-car
with lipstick.

his wife actually did
kick the bucket
when i was ten

chuck went down the drain

replaced him
with a guy named steve.

steve didn't give a shit
what we did

he was too busy
driving around the trailer-park
on a gold-wing
swiveling eye-dick
to little girls.

a call to the ex wife at 10:27pm

what was
the stuff
you got me
that winter when
the backs of my knees
dried out?

cortisone,
she says.

ah cortisone
thank you.

that all
you needed?

remember
the first time
we went walking
at the
woodpecker trails?

don't
justin.

ok
i'm sorry.

go to bed.

ok.

goodnight.

goodnight.

my seven hours as a door to door vacuum cleaner salesman

shake a stick
throw a jab
sodomize a garbage can.

peel an orange
lop off your foot with a banjo
play the cymbal with your penis.

wear a suit of baloney
snorkel on a gravel road
read a biography of michael jackson.

buy a 56inch sony flat-screen
bury it in your back yard.

start an email petition
to save the yeti.

sponsor your toaster
in a 5k run
to raise money
for chicken-pox research.

peel an orange
shake a stick
throw a jab
sodomize a garbage can.

raw motherfuckin' business

tippet
comes up to the work release control desk
with a polaroid
of a pimped out yellow impala:
says he's gonna
lay down
a dime piece on it
when he gets out.

he and my coworker
start spitting
indecipherable jargon:
glass pack,
bazooka amps,
cat and dual flowmaster,
bored out synchronized
redundancy valve intakes.

it's raw motherfuckin' business,
says tippet
handing the polaroid to my coworker.

raw motherfuckin' business,
says my coworker
and hands it to me.

it's a temporary distraction
from the metaphysical dilemma,
is what i want to say.

but you gotta
know your audience.

i tell him
it's raw
motherfuckin' business.

word,
says tippet.

i hand him the polaroid
and we
knock fists.

from the book of wtf?

sitting at the bar
trying to detach your mind
from the crucible
when she
taps your shoulder:

a tenth grade
high-school english teacher
named susan.

jesus your arm's
bigger around than my
thigh
hope you don't mean me harm,
she smiles
inviting you to
check the circumference
of her thigh.

you tell her
her smile
lights up
the catacombs
from greece
to ethiopia

which makes her face
turn red.

lets you
buy her
a bud-light

tells you
she's designing
a whole unit
on alice in wonderland.

you tell her
she needs to
do a unit on
carver and bukowski.

she's never heard
of either of them
but writes it down
on a napkin.

you tell her
you have to
empty
the contents of
your bladder.

so
creative with words,
she smiles
squeezes your neck
and says
hurry back.

not two minutes later
you do come back
and
she is gone.

gone brother.

nothing left

but her empty bud-light

and your
big
blue balls.

my grandfather

would not understand
this business of poetry
any more than my refusal
to go hunting with him
when i was old enough
to get a license.

but like then
he wouldn't judge
or slander
either.

carry on
carry on
old man river
charts our course,
is what
he would say
were he
still around.

then he'd
take a plug off his flask
squeeze my shoulder
with that big hand
torn apart
by a korean grenade

and ask
if i was putting it
to any long legged
brown-eyed
songs.

such is the charm
and global empathy
of the
inveterate drunk.

asking after a coworker

his secretary nancy told me don's doin well as to be expected
says he's been drivin helen's car
cause pullin up the driveway in his pickup
an seein her car there
it's just too much
havin to remember
she's gone.

wednesday mornings at the waveland

give me
an old iron-haired man
paper skin
yellow like an onion
and a fused left ankle
from a drunk driving accident
in nineteen fifty-seven.

it's bullshit

and he knows it's bullshit

the whole matinee
of infrastructure.

he won't let you
buy him whiskey

just the next
can of schlitz.

you know better
than to
talk his ear off:

standing in the shadow
of this monument
to the paradox
is enough.

sometimes
after five
or six

he'll talk about his
dead wife
ruth.

and on
very rare occasions
he sings
with the jukebox:

something low
almost imperceptible
from the throat.

it runs up
and through you
like a knife.

write through it

the failed marriage

the first case of gonorrhea
at thirty-one years old

the forty year old girlfriend
with a masters in quilting
who cuts her wrists
when you leave her

the three week case of
writers block

the seven week case of
writers block

a moth
the size of a pancake
on your bathroom mirror

bruises
the shape of
a woman's fist
up and down
your sternum

at 11:37am
on a tuesday

when your three year old son
turns to you
like a willing disciple
between bites of a peanut butter sandwich
and asks
why you don't
live at his house
anymore.

sipping a screwdriver at the ghetto bar half mile from my house

i've never been here before

but a young black
was shot and killed
out in the parking-lot
three days ago.

second shooting in six months.

city council's holding an emergency meeting
next thursday

going to shut them down permanent.

figured i'd check it out
before it becomes another empty building
on douglas avenue
plastered with realtor signs.

split down the middle
blacks and bosnians

occupancy sign says forty-five
which is a joke

more than that
around three pool tables
against the back wall.

bartender tells me
he's sitting alright
has a job lined up
selling cars
over in boone.

hit the second screwdriver
laying down the tip
when a heavy-set mulatto

trashed out of her skull
taps me on the shoulder.

my friends think you're an under-cover cop,
she says
lips barely moving
talking from a pinpoint
miles behind her eyes.

she manages to point out
the table full of
50cent rap-video
rejects
throwing me heavy
brow.

doesn't take good taste
to pull the trigger,
i think to myself
and ask how i can prove
i'm not a cop.

take some shots off my tits,
she says
pulling a
sloppy-bazooka out.

bartender
pours three test tubes
full of lemon-drops.

down
they go.

the first time i met my uncle from tennessee

he handed me a flask
in the church parking lot
prior to my aunt's funeral.

started telling me
how he's a functional alcoholic:

- never drinks before six pm
- never drives drunk
- rarely blacks out

then he told me
i talked
just like my dad did
when he was my age:

like some walking dictionary,
he said.

growing up
my father rarely spoke at all

and when he did

his vocabulary
was that of a plumber.

i asked
what happened to him
how growing up
it always seemed like
something had
sucked all the life out of him.

you
your sister
and your mom
is what happened to him.

that and
he stopped drinking
when he was forty seven years old
the poor dry bastard,
he said
and took the empty flask
from my hand

popped the trunk
of his rental car

and filled it back up.

3:38am at the truck stop

he sat down
at the little
u-shaped counter
up front

tried lighting
a cigarette
but kept dropping
the matches.

his skin
was the color of
skim milk.

you alright?
waitress
asked.

having
a heart attack,
his voice came
like a skeleton

sweat dripping
off his chin.

waitress
ran to the phone
for an
ambulance.

want me
to help you
onto the floor?
i asked him.

just light my cigarette
will you,

he said
body stiff
as a bent nail.

he took off
an old silver watch
with a white face
slid it towards me
along with his cellphone
and wallet.

you tell her
i remember that night
under the stars
at lake red rock,
he said

made me
write it
on a napkin
along with his
wife's phone number
down in
joplin missouri.

it's like you don't care about anything

i could
blow my head off with a shotgun
right here in front of you
or bake you a cake
or suck you off
and it'd all be the same to you
it's like you don't care about anything
she's standing there
in my underwear
uncorked jug of port wine in her left hand
not angry
just drunk poking my insides
i gently tell her
she has the wrong song
how i care about everything
i care so much
i took the time to find out
there's nothing to be done
about any of it
nothing to be done?
you're so fatalistic she says
i tell her i'm inviolable like an orchid
in-vi-o-lable?
christ
i think you use those big words
because you're afraid to let people in
i think your knees
are a national treasure i say
reaching out
running the back of my hand over her skin
her name's tiffany
works as a waitress at the lone-star steakhouse
reads ayn rand
experiencing a crisis of her christian faith
i'm falling for you
slowly like a feather
she says
sliding perpendicular
into my lap.

if you can believe it

i worked part time
in a daycare
freshman year
of college.

mainly i
stood on my head
and otherwise
hammed it up
for the little people.

this tractor
of a withered
bulgarian vulture
worked the infant room,
she had eyes in
the back of her head,
anytime i took a
little girl
to the bathroom
she appeared
stood in the doorway
until we finished.

must always keep
door open,
she'd say
even though
i always did.

three weeks in
the director
called me to her office,
they were cutting hours
due to a downtick in enrollment
(which was a lie)
but she'd call me
when things picked up.

i called bogdana
out to the fence
where my bicycle
was locked.

i'm not a pervert,
i told her
and explained
i was a student
in the college of education
trying to get some experience.

she didn't say anything

just lit a cigarette.

i unlocked my bike
working a
wad of spit
for the
north end
of her
forehead.

maybe you are
not a bad man,
she exhaled,
but you are confused
working here.

having no argument
with that,
i swallowed,
told her no hard feelings
and
pedaled off.

cala lilies in the east

i've never dreamt of cala lilies in the east

or a virgin indian princess
legs swung over a canoe
under a harvest moon.

it's never a maserati
redlining down the autobahn while
doing lines of coke off my pinkie nail
and getting head
from a bone-white eyed
fifteen year old
senegalese
model.

it's usually
all my teeth falling out
in the bathroom sink,

or,
for the third night
in a row now:

my scrotum swelling

torn open
by an army of black widow spiders
marching down my legs
two by two
into the power outlet.

my trick

back then
i could broad-jump
on top of anything:
trunks of cars,
washers and dryers,
even table-topped a honda gold wing once.
in those days i was one seventy-five
four percent body fat,
legs like zeus
from riding my bicycle three hundred miles a week.
my trick
was to pull out a bar stool
and bet a drink
i could hop up there
in one clean slice.
today, two-forty and one bad knee,
i resurrected the magic:
half bottle of black velvet in my left hand
i had air enough to clear the kitchen table
but my left foot kissed the lip.
flat on my back
watching a silverfish cut diagonally across the ceiling
my two dogs standing over me
sniffing for death.
see here gentleman, i said
showing them the bottle of black velvet.
it was unmolested,
my thumb corked in there tight
throughout the tumble of melee. my
new trick.

progression of a body through knives

just so you know
i've met someone
i really like him
things are getting serious

we agreed
so i'm letting you know
i'll be introducing him
to ivan
soon,
says your
ex wife
into the phone.

you knew
this day
was coming

thought you
might handle it
with aplomb
and sphinx
wisdom

hell
you've had
three relationships
and a cascade of
one night stands
in the year and a half
you've been divorced.

but you
hang up
the phone

a final door
closed

something substantial
draining
from your
face.

new overnight waitress at the truck stop

has me all
figured out:

i'm either
a homeland security agent
on long-term
detail

or with
the state police
collecting intelligence
for a drug or
prostitution ring.

probably
got this
whole place bugged
don't ya?
she asks
looking up
at the
light fixture.

i tell her
it's nothing like that

i'm just
lacking in all
practical
ambition

&

this is
a good place
to loaf
and write

dirty
limericks.

no
i can read people
like a book.
but don't worry hon
it's our secret,
she says
and squeezes my shoulder
finger zips her lip
and promises
to keep eyes
and ears
open.

then she
cups her hands
over her mouth
like an
amphitheater:

you all
got a friend
in pauline,
she calls up
to the
light-fixture.

my grandmother used to read to me

she'd get up
often
and walk out
to the
porch.

i was
nine
before i
caught on

but i didn't
say anything
about it
then.

ten years later
sitting with her
in the kitchen
a few months
after grandpa
died
from liver
cancer

she started
out
there.

you don't need
to hide it,
i said.

she brought the
bottle of gin
out.

we both

drank.

she got a
cardboard box
from the sewing
closet.

showed me
yellowed editorials
she'd written
for the local paper
forty years ago.

she said
working as a secretary
for the co-op
and supporting an
alcoholic
wasn't what she'd planned
for life.

did you know
his repair shop
never once
turned a
profit?

marrying your grandfather
was the single
worst thing
i ever
did,
she said
and tottered
off the
chair.

i scooped her
off the

floor

carried her
up the
stairs

and

tucked her
in.

wait long enough

you realize
nobody has a skeleton key
to the starving one winged bluebird
babbling and
smearing its own feces
on the walls of your heart.

or if there is a somebody
it's probably a
fourteen year old lebanese hooker
shackled to a sink
in an executive bathroom
somewhere in china

or a ninety year old
scandinavian glass blower
about to be hit by a bus
in estonia

or a one eyed
pygmy princess
sacrificed to the gods
three hundred years ago.

wait long enough
you give up on the concept
completely

you start dreaming of origami woodchucks
garden gnomes swimming the english channel
or digging your own grave
with the blunt edge of a hatchet.

your mind goes
cream puff egg yolk through a straw

but you no longer much
care:

you write poems about it
2:17 in the morning
huddled in a booth at the flying j
festooned with flasks of bourbon
trying to remember
what it was
that one girl told you she had.
the one with a tattoo of a watch on her wrist
said she was half irish half dingo
how she was going to tie you to her bed
but she took off while you were in the pisser.
what the fuck was it?
ah yes–

fibromyalgia.

the trucker's wife

lined up three shots
of black velvet
cupped them in her palm
and downed the batch.
it's my birthday baby
let me kiss you
on the cheek,
she said
pulling me into her.

hey man
don't mind my wife,
young guy my age
slid me his hand.
said he was will
and that was veronica.
told me
he ran flatbed for jb hunt
but they wouldn't let his dog
ride with him
so he was looking
for a new outfit.

it's my birthday,
veronica grabbed me,
i wanna dance
but he won't act the fool
you act the fool
with me?

you don't have to man
but you got my blessing,
will said.

suzy q's
isn't a dancing bar
and on top of that
tuesday is pool league

but we got out there
between tables.
i was the only thing
holding her up,
barely at that.

they humored us
for a couple minutes
then brian
the bartender
whistled me off.

i'm gonna
tell you my secret,
she whispered
as we sat back down.
she pulled
a plastic prosthetic
out of her bra,
my right tittie's
only half size,
she said
and started crying.

hey that's
nothing
you're a pretty girl,
i said and
put my hand on her shoulder
(she was
looked a little like cher
with a slight paunch
and bug eyes).

you're good people,
she said
and put her arm
around me.

then she turned another
black velvet trifecta
fell off her stool
and cracked her head
on the wall.

that's it,
brian said
and told them
get the hell out.

will and i
put an arm on each shoulder,
halfway to the car
she started kicking,
i ain't getting
in that damn car
it's my birthday
goddammit.

sorry about this man,
will said
as veronica pulled off a heel
and chucked it
at the bar window.
he wasn't in much
better shape than her
and i wasn't far behind.

don't worry man
just get her home
before the cops come.

we wrestled her
into the passenger side
of his little two-seater
and i held the door closed
from the outside
while he got in.

drive safe,
i called
through the window.

he gave me thumbs up
got it reversed
and started out of the lot
when she opened the door
and rolled out
onto the cement.

don't ever ask me how
we got her onto my lap
in his passenger seat.

you damn dirty dogs
damn damn dirty dogs,
she screamed
digging her nails into my forearm
as will swung wide
up and over the curb
and we pulled out
into it.

turbo

lived at
the group foster home
in ames.

he had large orange
hearing aids

his voice came like
an echo through molasses.

they called him turbo
because every time
someone flicked a lighter
or struck a match
he'd sprint away like a quarter horse
while they all laughed.

i found myself next to him
on the city bus
sophomore year
of high school.

he told me
his real name
was alex.

said he was twenty years old
and when he graduated high-school
next year
he was going to china
to find his parents.

he didn't know
their names
or where they lived.

said
he'd just start
knocking on doors.

how i learned

we were
in the middle
of john kearn's
fallow bean field.

grandpa
strapped wooden blocks
to the gas and brake
of his suburban
with bungee.

he showed me the gist
and where to stomp
the emergency-brake
if i lost nerve.

then he got out

said certain things
a man needs to figure
alone.

sweat
ran from my asshole
but i feathered the thing

worked it
in a big slow circle.

my nerve didn't go,
i took it faster,
made a figure eight
and nosedived
clean into the little creek
on the south edge.

grandpa set his flask down
put his hand on my back,

said a man usually
gets thrown by his first bull,
that i'd done well.

said it would be some time
before john kearn came back
from the indian casino
to pull us out
with his tractor.

we sat in the sand
next to the creek.

he gave me a small
taste
of the flask,
told me someday
i'd want to ride a woman
like i'd done the
suburban

how the results
might be similar

but i shouldn't
let that
deter me.

ivan #16

yesterday
your mother and i
met for lunch
at the drake diner.

she gave me
a tear stained letter.
it said
the failure of our marriage
was the greatest tragedy
of her life.

someday
you will despise me
for breaking her heart.

but this afternoon
we chased geese
at greys lake
whooping like madmen
until our voices
went hoarse.

when i
dropped you off
at your mother's

you perched
at the living room window
like an owl

and blew me
a kiss.

childish things

my grandfather
kept a silver zippo
next to an ashtray
in the upstairs
bathroom.

when i visited
as a young boy
the first thing i did
was go up there and
flick it on
for a quick second:

the true beginning
of fishing
hunting
and wood-shop projects
that kept me
too excited to sleep
for
weeks in advance.

he's been gone
for years

but i still
go up there
when i can find the time
to pay grandma
a visit.

the zippo
is gone

replaced
by a
cheap green
bic.

i run my hand
over top of
the ashtray

remembering
what it was
before the world
bared it's teeth.

only waitress at the truck stop who never uses the cash register

pamela
is half indian

grey-black hair
in a double braid
down her back.

every time
she serves me
another waitress
rings the ticket.

i figured
she was slow
or bad with numbers

maybe had a
theft charge
in her past.

but yesterday
on my way out
she was sitting
on the
hood of her car
smoking a
cigarette.

come here a sec
tell me
what this says,
she motioned over
and handed me
a white piece of paper
creased in thirds.

told me
she found it

taped to her
apartment door
that morning.

i told her
it was a note
from her landlord
saying she had
five business days
to get rid of
her dog.

she stood up
and snuffed out
the cigarette
with her heel.

bear's been
with me
since idaho,
she said
and walked back in
leaving the note
in my hand.

my grandfather was a deadeye

he dropped pheasants
at eye-level,
doves with a pistol,
quarters thrown in the air
for shots of whiskey.

after he passed
dad got his old
double barrel shotgun

lucy.

she hung
from two lengths of twine
in the basement
until i was fourteen.

i bought a box
of slug-shot
from wal-mart,
no note,
popped one in the left chamber
barrel in my throat
big toe on the trigger.

click.

i'd accidentally
had the
thumb-lever
set for
the right barrel.

sometimes i still hear it
in my dreams

a dropped spoon
on the kitchen floor

or a nail gun
dancing on a roof
off in some
distance.

in iraq

my husband is in iraq,
she said
between sucks of a dark drink
through a thin yellow straw.

the house
smelled of babies milk
and potpourri.

their black lab
licked my hand
while she paid
the baby sitter.

i've never done this before,
she said.

me either,
i lied.

grocery shopping for the schizophrenics

my first job out of college
was as a mental health counselor
at a non-profit
in iowa city

four clients
lived at the residential house
on birch street

every wednesday
i had 150$
to buy groceries

i never made a budget
but i always got what was needed
with enough left over for

james' king size snickers
marlboro reds for carol
kim's tube of cookie dough

and a cosmo
for sarah

because she was studying to be an actress
in hollywood
for when god stopped fucking with her.

if we ever meet

when we shake hands
mine will make a loud clicking sound
i'll tell you i broke it in a bar fight
and it healed badly
which is a lie
what happened is
i went into the woods behind brookside park
with a bottle of whiskey
it was the summer of two-thousand and four
and i was living in my parent's basement
why i went into the woods that day
i don't know
but there i was
sitting on a log getting good and numb
then i punched that tree three times hard
pretending it was my own face.

the qc lady

drove around the plant
in a joystick controlled wheelchair
because multiple sclerosis
was erasing
important parts of her spine.
there were two internet stations
in the break-room
of hach chemical:
five in the morning before the five-thirty shift
i'd be playing at poet
while mellisa scrolled various horoscopes
looking for reasons not to drink
that gallon of bleach
she always talked about
after too many tequilas
at the foxhead
on friday nights.

hum in the belly of the spider

schools
hardware stores
the big insurance companies downtown
even wal-mart
and the post office
are closed.

i tuck my jeans
inside my boots
and trudge
half a mile
through knee deep snow
to a cafe.

a line
of purple neon
along the perimeter
of the ceiling
flickers
on and off.

i order a long island

then another.

out the window
an armada of snow plows
come and go
in waves of three.

i try to
imagine myself
five years down the road

two years

next month.

then my ex wife
sends a text message:

today is a day i
wish you were
still here.

ten and two

jackie
was my
supervisor
at allied.

stilted
awkward

something was
missing or broken

and i liked her
for it.

but other coworkers
complained.

one day
the unit manager
brought jackie
into a conference room
with me and my coworkers
for a skill building session
to get to
know her
better.

she told us
both her father
and brother
had committed suicide
she suffered from
severe depression
and was having
electroshock therapy.

shortly after
they told her

she could take a demotion
or get fired.

she left.

that was
seven
years ago.

today
reading the paper
at a burrito joint
i looked up
to see her walk in.

she ate
and left
in about
twenty minutes.

i finished
the paper
and left
about half
an hour
after that

got in the car
turned it over
glanced right
saw her there
four cars down
hands ten and two
on the wheel.

she just sat there
ten and two
for the longest time.

then softly
put her head
down
on the wheel.

down at the alpine tap

jimmy the bartender
tells me
the difference
between men and women
is that a man
rolls out of bed
just to
roll out of bed

but a woman
won't get up
without a reason.

i know
he lives with
his
eighty-seven
year old mom. i
ask him
why she gets up
in the morning.

i suppose
soap operas
and me. but
i don't
spend enough
time with her,
he says
cleaning out
a row of shot glasses
with a wash cloth.

why don't you
spend more
time with
her?

no
now there you go
trying to make me
feel guilty.

sorry
jimmy.

you got a
special way
you know that,
he says
pulls out his cellphone
and tells me
watch the bar
for a minute.

can you fly emily?

randy halsrud called out loudly to my sister
from back of the bus.

i was sitting near the front,
my sister was toward the middle.
the whole bus could hear it,
he said it three or four more times.

he was doing it
because my sister was severely overweight,
picked on all the time.

as her older brother
i should have stood up for her.

but i just stared out the window,
holding my breath
and counting telephone poles
as they went by.

in the hallway after taking a piss

three large portraits
hang on the wall
like sentinels.

they're my age
maybe a
little older.

all three
in crisp
police uniforms:

dump trucks
for jaws

mirthless
pale blue eyes
like genocide.

they'd
gut me
like a deer
if they knew
what i was
up to.

get your
tight little butt
back in here,
gloria calls
from the bedroom.

yes mam,
i say
and salute
and apologize
for what i'm about to do
to their mother

for the
third time
tonight.

what i like about you justin

you're the first white dude
i met
doesn't take their job
so dead all serious hell
straight down
through the root
you're more black
than half
the brothers
i know.

the mad scientist

started doing speedballs
at the age of ten
after running away from home
because his father
beat him.

he waits tables
at i-hop

gets back to work-release
around midnight

gives
what co's call

—long ear—

most of them
avoid him.

i let him
ramble on about
a world without currency

the benefits of
vigilante justice

and

what a
woman's role
should be.

last night he
taught me proper technique
for grabbing a motherfucker
by the throat.

like this,
he said
pinching my windpipe
with his fingertips.

whose leading who then
huh?
he let loose his
boiler laugh

slapped the control desk counter

and told me

i was good people.

which amongst
these guys

is the
highest compliment.

at the 24 hour laundry

there's a kid
sitting cross-legged
under a
pinball machine.

he's scratching
the end
of an opened
wire hanger
against the
wall.

wanna play?
i lean under
and ask.

i'm not tall enough,
he says.

sure you are,
i get a
chair.

he works the left flipper
and i work the
right.

it's a simpsons
machine.

you watch simpsons?
i ask.

i don't watch cartoons
i only watch
wwe,
he says
and slams a fist

as we lose
a ball.

he's got a face
like a badger

looks underfed
a little grey
in the skin.

you here
by yourself?
i ask.

mom's out there,
he says
pointing to
a tore up
train-wreck
in cut-off jeans
sharing a cigarette
with a moon-faced
pile of bones.

who's the
guy?

i don't know
him,
he says.

jonathan!
get out here,
his mom
calls.

she
gets in a rusted out
taurus

with the guy
and drives off.

mom says
she'll be back
in an hour,
he says
and flashes a five
and slides it
into the
quarter machine.

sitting alone at the authentic mexican restaurant

a young family
in the booth behind me.

the daughter:

pale-faced

about my son's age.

she stands up

turns around

little finger tapping my shoulder
she asks:
where's your family?

abby
your father said
sit down,
her mother says
plopping her back
into the booth.

but
where's his family?
she asks.

probably at home
or at the store
now sit down
and eat your dinner,
her father says.

no my child
they are not at home
or at the store

i pissed them
down the drain.

but things

transitory
cheap
and lurid
as they are:

i'll string something else
soon enough.

currently
four different single mothers
are tripping over each other
to lash themselves
and their children
to this
jalopy frame of mine.

i pretend
they're not just after
the health insurance
and security
of my state job

they pretend
i'm not just after
the hockey puck
between their legs.

their children
watch us
very closely:

apprentices
to it all.

there goes the big brazilian

five years ago
he was
in work release
for breaking
into storage units
to support
a heroin addiction.

2am
and 4am count
i'd often find him
upright
in his bunk
rocking slowly
back and forth
like a metronome.

said
he started doing it
as a kid
in his
third or fourth
foster home.

silly
i know
silly thing
for a grown man
to do,
is what
he told me
back then.

lanky
like a cat.

there he goes
down crocker

past the
coffee shop window
in a
light rain.

at the q on a wednesday afternoon in december

practicing bank shots
at a table
in the far corner.

two workers
were at a table across from me
taking measurements
to re-felt it.

he looks like a college boy
ask him,
heavy-set guy in overalls
said to his partner.

they were arguing over
eight times seven.

fifty-six,
i said. but
i hadn't snapped it off rote
had to work back
knowing eight and five was forty
and add sixteen to that:

i'd been in remedial math
all the way through high-school.

whole episode broke my concentration
it was pay by the hour
grabbed the rack of balls
headed for the bar.

take it easy,
i gave them
pistol-wrist.

hope we didn't run you off,
said his partner

younger guy
white-sox pullover
adam's apple of horse.

not at all,
i said
headed downstairs
handed the bartender
the rack of balls
and ordered
a rum and coke.

i was a college boy–

didn't feel like it though,
didn't have that paradigm of ambition
that supercilious eye
those base-ten blueprints–
but i knew their words
and liked the women
at their house parties.

i came from people like those two upstairs
but wasn't one of them either
though i preferred their company
over the other type.

i finished the rum and coke
thinking how
i didn't belong
much of anywhere.

i liked that.
i liked that a-lot.

i ordered another
rum and coke
and a
shot of tequila.

single mothers, little brown assholes like buttons

amber
pulled me out of tuesday night karaoke
at the plaza pub
three weeks ago.

tonight
her daughter stays with grandma
and we sit on her couch
drinking from
a bottle of grey goose.

her tv
is the size of a buffalo.
i talk her into turning it off
and we listen to
the oldies station
on the radio.

what are
your thoughts?
i ask her.

she says she
has no thoughts.

inclinations?

none of those either.

what's on your mind?
she asks
running her hand
through my hair.

i tell her
we've failed
and been failed
but somewhere inside of us

a hamster
runs his wheel
willing us on.

she says
i'm crazy
but
likes the way i talk.

sanguine
from the vodka
i tell her
her little brown asshole
looks like a button.

whatever!
her face goes red
and she playfully
kicks my leg
with her left foot.

the year is 2009.

god is
long dead.

but the hamster

cunning like trigonometry

wills us on.

my first time

the sound of pee
against metal
shook me
from
black sleep.

the jail urinal
was directly
behind my
head.

you were
plenty rotten
when they
brung you in,
a sandpaper-faced bum
laughed
while shaking off.

i pulled the
stiff sheet
over my head
and fell
back.

when i woke
the bum was
gone -

i noticed the
ceiling was
pink.

the control door
buzzed open.

young guy
my age

shoulders
wide as a picnic table
and hair-trigger
bear traps
in his eyes.

he jerked
the jailer's hand
off his shoulder
and sat on the bench
across from me.

i've thrown
plenty men
more than you
against that window,
he said
without looking
at me.

he started peeling
the nail
of his middle finger
back from the bed
and let blood
drip down
on the
cement floor.

names jacob,
he said.

i'm justin,
i said.

he asked me
if i knew
how volcanoes
killed off

the
dinosaurs.

before i could answer
he told me
all about it
how his dad
was an expert
on volcanoes
right before he
committed suicide
with a shotgun
when jacob
was twelve
they were planning
a trip to
mount st. helens.

if it ever
goes again
i'll be standing
at the lip,
he said with
tears in his
eyes.

he apologized
for crying
told me today
was his dad's
birthday.

how he always
got spun out
on dope
on dad's
birthday.

my newest client at work release

stabbed correctional officers
with pens
on two separate occasions
while in prison.

he's in my office right now
twirling a bic
between his fingers
telling me the arson charges
were bullshit.

he'd been living
with his aunt
but she kicked him out
for smearing shit
on his bedroom walls.

the only reason
i set that fire
on her sidewalk
was to keep warm.

guy's a full blown schizo,
doesn't belong here,
but the prisons
are overcrowded.

i should ask for the pen
in a calm voice.

i should always have
another parole officer
in the office
when i meet with
this guy.

but i just stare
at the pen

like a golden-ticket.

wishing he'd snap
and make me
the trifecta.

i could parlay it
into a month off
paid.

maybe early retirement
and a lump-sum payment
if he buries it
in my eye.

standing in line to buy lighter fluid and a bic

the cavanaugh house
is an old
army barracks
behind the
airport
where people
with no insurance
go to
die.

mr. arnold's
been in
two months
with cancer
of the stomach.

i got the call
today

went down
over lunch break
for a doctor's signature
so i could
close out
his parole file.

he'd strong-armed a bank
in seventy-seven
week after
dropping out
of the
tenth grade.

did thirty years

got out this june

lived at the y

and ran stock
at the goodwill warehouse
for a month
before he started
coughing up
chunks of
intestine.

i'd check on him
every other week

he'd always remind me
to burn that cardboard box
with all his possessions
at the foot of his bed
after the reaper
passed
through.

it's not much
a fool's bounty
but my brother down in keokuk
won't claim me
and i don't want the sharks
picking through
my bones,
he'd say
forcing a smile.

when my father dies

we're little more
than strangers

but i do know
neither of us
owns a suit.

i'll have to
take some of his clothes
to my ex-wife:

she's good
with
those things:

she'll write down
his measurments
on a
piece of paper:

she'll ask
to go with me:

but i'll go
to the outlet store
in the mall
alone.

i'll hand the
piece of paper
to a clerk
and tell them
i need a
medium priced
brown suit

(his father
was buried

in a
brown suit)

then i'll have them
measure me
for something cheap
in black.

for the matriarch

my grandmother
is half an hour late
to everything.

my mother
is half an hour early
to everything.

i split the difference
and show up
ten minutes early.

but great grandma

she had it right.

she didn't
go to THINGS

or bother with
the intransigent calumny
of people.

she tended garden

read encyclopedias

national geographic

and drew pictures
of spiders.

she kept her gallstones
in a pickle jar
on her coffee table

and the little
homemade sign

nailed to her front door
said:

absent neighbors
make good
fences.

the place-mat at the vietnamese restaurant

informed me
my oriental zodiac
is the horse

it went on
expostulating
on my
psychological makeup

the final
sentence of which
has stuck
with me
three days now:

you need people,
it said
in simple
5point
font.

i'm not sure
why it
took me
thirty-two years
and a place-mat
to fully realize
a fundamental sickness
in me.

i do
need people.
i've been denying it
from a
young age

throwing them off
as if

letting people in
was a weakness.

this is
a revelation
worth noting

something to
bounce off a
trusted friend.

but of course
tonight
on the porch
during a rainstorm

i have no one
to tell it to
but this
bottle of beer.

i used to get so very lonely

i was
a young bank examiner
drunk beyond repair
in downtown chicago.

i stumbled north
where the broken pavement
reeked
of open sewers
and the homeless
were putting down for the night
in bus stops and
alleys.

the street vendor
sold me a fifth
of whiskey
and let me piss
behind his car.

don't get lost
around here,
he called after me.

a shattered
black woman
sat on the steps
of a rotting
apartment
building.

she
nodded.

i
nodded
back.

sexes?
she whispered
patting the space
beside her.

i
sat.

she
put her arm
over
my shoulder.

for twenty dollars
we could go
upstairs
and i could do
whatever.

all i wanted
was to talk
for a bit
and
get to know
her view
of the world.

she looked at me
like i'd just
shit in her lap
and said
if we wasn't gonna fuck
get the hell on
cause she had mouths
to feed.

she said i danced like a black man

how
she only ran
with blacks

but maybe tonight
would be
the exception.

i stuffed
a shot glass
between her tits
and asked
why she only made it
with blacks.

she ran her tongue
into my ear

told me how
white men
over-think
the world.

she said
it guts them
and they are left
with no sensuality
for their women.

i told her
that sounded like racism

how maybe
it had more to do
with the individual
than skin color.

she

patted
my dick

said
i just proved
her point

and

took my pussy
back to
the dance floor.

what's the numbers bro?

the big mexican
is the only coworker
who knows
i write poetry.

regret
telling him.

all he ever
wants to know
is how many books
i've sold.

doesn't believe
i don't know

that i've never
asked the publisher.

nine-hundred-and-fifty-thousand
by the end of the year
you're gonna blow up bro
i can feel it,
is what he says.

i tell him
the odds of anyone
selling nine-hundred-and-fifty-thousand
books of poetry
are about as good as
all his wet-back brethren
sprouting wings
and voluntarily
flying back south for the winter.

nah bro
you're gonna blow up
hiroshima,

he says
holding out his fist.

i knock it
for the same reason
you stare
at a car wreck.

we go back to
video footage
on his cell phone:

bug-eyed moped
sucking him off
behind daytona's.

look at her
take that gak,
he smiles
holding out the fist
again.

yahtzee,
i say
clearing his fat knuckles
out of my air-space.

yahtzee
motherfucking yahtzee
you're off the chain bro,
he laughs
and pulls up
some still shots
of what he calls
donkey asses
from karaoke
last tuesday
at the plaza pub.

sitting on the curb of the square in memphis mo

high school kids
and twenty-somethings
carved a
slow continuous parade
out of the 3/4 mile loop
past gerth hardware,
cooks men's store,
lionel's tap (where my
dad and uncle dick were)
and the
dollar general.

my older half sister
was explaining
why she hated
uncle dick
and simultaneously
trying to get the attention
of two flat-tops
in varsity jackets
driving a pickup
with ridiculously
large wheels.

every time they
came by
she'd tell me shut up
puff her lips out
suck in her cheeks
and arch her back.

as i was trying
to find a pattern
in the girls
hopping
from one car
to another a
confederate flag headband

buzzed us
popping a wheelie
down the sidewalk
on his three wheeler.

the flat-tops
stopped in front of us
whistled
and my half-sister
jumped in
they hooked a right
off the loop
down towards the river.

i stood up
dusted my hands off
on my pants thinking

well

here's one more place
i don't
belong.

to all the roommates i've ever had (newsletter #1)

i'm sorry
about all the homeless people
i let sleep
on your nice couches

and the strange women
brought home from bars:

matt,
remember the ethiopian
presidential candidate
with eight inch toenails
and the surprise
he left in our
microwave?

tavis,
how about the girl
with a purple vagina
on her elbow
and the
smurf shaped stain
she left on the
living room carpet?

some of you
still email me:

i know i rarely respond

but like antelopes
escaping from quicksand

your messages
please me.

george,
you always said

i should be a
philosopher

well

i did you one better
on the scale of
diminishing
human utility:

i've become a writer of poetry

and a daily drinker
to keep it
in check.

i've got a
two year old son

he holds my heart
like a toy airplane.

had a wife for a little while

but like most of you
she wised up.

yours truly
amidst sardine eyes
and piccolos
to the east,
justin joseph hyde.

in a low mood

on the couch with a beer

your mind stuck somewhere
between quicksand
and lead paint.

your son
playing with matchbox cars
on the linoleum floor
of the kitchen
suddenly announces:
look daddy!
look at me!

up to the tops of his legs
like a fisherman's
waders

he's gotten
your work boots
on his tiny feet

trudging toward you
with the concentration
of warfare.

it's nothing much

i'm sure every father has seen it.

but you smile

truly smile

for the first time this week.

i didn't write any poems last night

my three year old son
kept crawling out
from beneath the blanket
serving as a door to the bedroom
to inform me:

daddy
there's a
monster under the bed.

we peered under the bed
flexed our muscles
and shouted:

go home
go home
and feed your fish!

this usually does the trick.

but not last night.

last night
all that consoled
was my continued presence
on the floor.

i was a good sentinel
for about twenty minutes.

then i fell asleep.

woke up this morning
on my stomach:

ivan
slung over my back

sleeping soundly
like a small bear.

the babysitter

my mother
worked her way
through nursing school
by emptying bed pans
at a nursing home.

she ran the emergency room
at mary greely
for twenty three years

until she got caught
skimming vicodin

lost her license

and started buying it
off an old friend of mine.

your mom
owes me five hundred bucks,
he says.

look at her
in that rocking chair
wringing her hands.

she's fifty three now

works front desk
at motel six
for eight fifty an hour.

i tried Justy,
she stares at the floor
after i flush another
bag.

ivan can't be alone with grandma

she wouldn't do it
on purpose
but when she's taking twelve a day
instead of the two prescribed
it's cold turkey for a week
till the script gets refilled
and she'd have him in the hospital
with some fake illness
trying to get a script for him or
sneaking around
begging it off patients and
visitors
or stealing it out of a purse
i've seen her
at the bottom
rocked my mom back and forth on the couch
pale skin
sweating through a sheet.

sitting in a mcdonald's booth at 2am

for a little guy
he's got big arms,
the girlfriend says to the boyfriend
about the guy running the
cash-register.

he's probably on some
strength drugs
this is all natural baby,
he says
and rolls up his sleeve
and puts very little tension
on a barbed wire tattoo.

i'm just sayin',
she says
and spits chew in a cup.
for a little guy
he's got big arms.

what? you wanna fuck him
or what?

no honey
i was just sayin'.

he belches in her face.
just say that,
he says.

she
laughs

the hummingbird
blinks

a gopher just surfaced
somewhere in china

my wife and son
left me
two weeks ago

and

the guy
behind the cash-register
has big arms
for a little guy.

i'll do it myself daddy

even the grizzled
old truckers

withered gargoyles
who rarely speak
or move at all
while leaning over
their food.

even they smile
like peeled bananas

when my little boy
not even three years old

trudges across the
truck stop restaurant

dragging back
a high chair
twice
his size.

a dull lady with big calves

buys me
a shot of tequila
at the twisted parrot
on a
tuesday night.

lynyrd skynyrd
on the
jukebox

she tells me
someday
she wants a house
on a cul-de-sac

three children

and a cache
of
snowmobiles.

staring listlessly
at the cubs
on the overhead tv

i wait for some lightning
smoke signals
any sign of life
or a little madness
out of her:

but all she says
is something
about her
thursday night
dart-league

&

a tick
the size of a walnut
she pulled off
her beagle.

i told myself
i wouldn't
fuck idiots
anymore:

but it seems
the world offers little
beyond dull ladies
with big calves.

i order us
a double of
black velvet.

she opens her cell-phone
and chortles
a chorus of zeros
into it.

i shoulder back
to check
her ass.

i wait

&

wait.

why i'm a morning person

a thin dirt trail behind our rented cabin at
lacey keosauqua state park
wound down a steep
rut covered
incline into the forest where
predawn
spider webs stuck to my lips
it veered
right towards shore then
all the way around
lake sugema
the half-way point was
marked by a moss
covered bridge spanning a
dry creek bed
my father
put me on his shoulders
climbed up onto the railing and
pointed through the oak trees
out across the still
water
past blue and white buoys lining the perimeter of
the swimming area
to the opposite shore line where
a wide staircase of cracked cement steps
swept up the side of the bank in a half moon crescent
the top half hidden by
morning fog so it looked
liked the stairs just wound
up into the sky
where do they go
i wanted to know
let's find out
he smiled
the smile he only ever
smiled before the sun was up
and his drinking
began in earnest.

before we stopped speaking to each other

my father and i
went for walks:

not around the block
or half hour hikes
in the woods:

we'd go on ten
fifteen milers:

an
all day affair.

that day
was a twelve miler
to the pizza buffet
and back.

halfway home
we passed a bike rack
in front of the mall.

would i
steal one of those bikes
if i was bone tired
and thirty miles from home?
he asked.

told him no
(i was eleven
and couldn't imagine
stealing anything)

he didn't
believe me:

told me
he'd stolen one

off an indian reservation
after a night of drinking
when he was
in the army.

well old man
if we spoke to each other
i'd tell you
you were right:

i've stolen bicycles
cars
kegs of beer
even a crossbow:

i've lied
cheated
and pissed on the hearts of women
like urinal cakes
with surprisingly little
remorse.

all those faces in high-school

none of them
were my friends

but
every strange sideways
beer-bong spatula click
of the spider clock
my mind
drifts back to that time

&

a somber
gun barrel blue note
grinds slow and sad
from the gut

until
the egg timer
embedded in my ankle
runs dry
and i side-arm another empty bottle
into the brick wall of my basement

&

go back to pretending
i always planned for it to be like this:

thirty years old
drunk
broke

alone
on a tuesday
10:43am
in des moines, iowa.

dad's underwear

in the hamper
peed in and
smeared with shit. mom said
he'd got sick with the flu again
while at uncle jim's
on saturday night.
jim isn't really my uncle,
he's dad's childhood friend.
dad partied at the bars with him a-lot
up in des moines
on the weekends.
by the time i was sixteen
i'd seen the bottom of enough whiskey
bottles to know why dad had really shit his pants.
but it took me twenty-six years
losing a woman that loved me
by cheating on her
before i really understood
why mom
always cried
like that.

when my dad sold the vw rabbit to three asians

he came home the next day
with a case of crown royal
and five silver bars.

they were the size
of a good shit
but heavy beyond reason.

i used them to build a fort
for my g.i. joes
but eventually he put them
on top of his dresser.

they collected dust
for the next twelve years

until i was coming off amphetamines
but didn't want to be.

i took the greyhound
home from college
in the middle of the day

climbed up there
and palmed one.

i had no idea
what it was worth.

when the coin dealer in solon
counted out twenty-five
twenty dollar bills
i went cotton mouth
and my pupils dilated.

it was gone in three days
of crank
and tainted vagina.

i think
i've apologized for it
more than once
over the phone
during times of severe impairment

but i can't remember

and we never talk.

not all women are cunts

we parked her car
in front of the old farmhouse
where i rented a room.

i'd picked her up at
denny arthurs
which is the old-folks bar in des moines
i often went to
when closing time approached
and i'd struck out
elsewhere.

i undid my pants

put her hand
on it.

she
worked it

then she put her head
down there.

then these
small
dry sobs.

told me
she was living
with a man

he was good
to her three kids.

she didn't love him

but he didn't deserve
this.

i pulled my pants up

watched her
drive away.

i flicked the kitchen lights on

cockroaches scurried
behind the stove
and down
the garbage disposal.

i sat quiet
at the kitchen table
for some time.

feeling very much
like one of
them.

watching my father walk out of a gas station

hands in pockets of a goodwill flannel
he stumbles slightly
off the lip of the curb.

dad used to be built like a mack truck,
now he's frail,
sixty-three years old:
walks with a minor limp
from a hit and run accident on his bicycle
twenty some years ago.

watching him now
(the wind might blow him away
like a plastic sack)
it's hard to imagine
i ever hated him.

growing up
i thought he was out to ruin my life.

but he's just a quiet private man,
never recovered after
losing his mother to cancer
at the age of thirteen.

my father never knew what to do with his hands,
let alone a son
and a crazy pill freak for a wife.

he leans in the door
says his eyes are tired
would i drive for a while.

i get in the driver's seat,
he hands me a toothpick
and we keep on driving
down to memphis missouri

to run the weed wacker
around his mother
and father's grave.

fishing with larry

first week here i lent my vacuum cleaner to
larry down the hall. an old crouton:
liver spots on his dome: said he was on ssdi for some heart
condition.
i didn't think much of it for a week.
then i knocked on his door. nothing.
then a door across the hall creaked open a few inches:
oh larry took you fishing didn't he?
came a female voice like cigarette smoke
doused in cat piss.
she told me you can't borrow nothing to larry
cause' he'll hawk it for nigger cocaine. i thanked her for the info
and asked if there were any other
procedural quirks i needed to know around here.
she said she didn't know what
procedural quirks was but
for a ten-spot
she'd eat my pud.

when i was eight

my grandfather
lived in an apartment
above gerth hardware
in memphis
missouri.

his doorknob
was a dull
white sphere
that popped off
into your hand
if you pulled
before turning.

a dried out
brown couch
sat against
the wall
in the living
room.

from there
i could see
into the bedroom
and further down
the bathroom.

dad picked him up
off the bed
and carried him
in his arms
to the bathtub.

no one spoke
while he
worked the washcloth
over his body.

afterward
dad sat in the chair
next to the
window.

his hands
disappeared
inside his hair
as he
stared
at the floor.

the only time i remember laughing with the old man

we were watching
a cheech
and chong movie.

they were siphoning gas
from a parked car
with a
length of hose.

cheech got some
in his mouth
while
getting it started.

i was young

five or six years old

didn't really understand
why we were laughing.

only that

it felt good.

it ain't all the same

now it ain't all the same
some are a nice tight little pocket
and some are like big paper sacks,
says my coworker shavon
using his hands for affect.

our other coworker mark
is a christian

he's courting a lady from florida
over the phone.

he's a virgin
and doesn't believe in sex
before marriage.

we're trying to help him
traverse
the actualities.

mark is
mortified
by the conversation.

shavon goes on:

all i'm sayin' is there's a difference
betcha' i ask justin right now
he remembers
the best piece he ever had.

i just nod.

i don't say anything.

but he's right.

i do remember

that cold december night

your mother's
bow walled trailer
in saint louis.

we knocked
your little sister's twin bed
clean off the frame. your red hair
heavy with sweat, across my chest.
we could see our breath
trailing up

and then disappearing
through a
crack in the wall.

at the pool table

my father
is one of the best shots
in the state.

that i found this out
at twenty-two
from a complete stranger
while drinking in a bar
on the other side of iowa
sounds about right
for dad and i.

i knew
he played a-lot.

i knew
they moved into town
after dad's mom died
when he was thirteen

that he
and uncle dick
spent a-lot of time in the tavern
even at that age
and learned to drink
and shoot.

that winter
home from college
during winter break
i asked him
if he wanted to
shoot a few racks.

everyone in the place
knew him
by his nickname—
buck.

don't pull any punches,
i said.

he didn't.
most games
it was over
if i missed a shot.

my mom was at home
fighting an addiction
to painkillers
that nobody
talked about.

she'd told me
at various times
how dad
felt like a failure in life.

but right then
at the pool table
it was fluid concentration.
people from the bar
came over
just to watch him shoot.

he didn't have to think
about the train-wreck wife
at home

that all he'd achieved
was becoming a
bug man
for presto-x

how his father
basically abandoned him
and his brother
after his mom died—

how my sister
and i
pretend
he doesn't exist.

in that four by eight foot space
at the pool table
my dad has a voice
and each game
is a clean slate.

on being asked about parental influence on my creative development as a child

my mother
brought home a birthday card
for my half-sister
down in missouri.

write something nice
for billie-joe,
she said
handing me the card
and a pen
as i sat in front of the tv.

that summer
i'd spent a week down in missouri
with billie-joe and her mother.
she'd introduced me
to all her friends:

there was frog
a star wars geek
who worked in the video store.

i doodled a picture of him
on the back of the card
with the caption:
use the force you must
happy birthday
from the frog.

then there was her boyfriend jared.
he was on steroids
wore ridiculously tight t-shirts
and was always asking people to
touch his guns.

i drew a picture of him
with the caption:

i know it's your birthday baby
but tell me
how's the flex?

then i did two or three others

filling up
most of the blank space.

my mother said:
you ruined the card.

she ripped it down the middle

tossed it in the garbage

and i was
sent to my room for the night.

god bless america

how you like
my new wheels?
asks larry.

he's leaning
on a push-cart walker
with hand breaks
and a small american flag
attached to the
front end.

tells me
he had another mini-stroke
last week
and the sawbones
saddled him
with this contraption.

he says:
i'm not afraid to die–
just ain't ready yet–
still like
standing out here
watching the ladies
walk by–
i smile and
they flirt with me.

i tell him
the ones
walking by
to the high-school
down the road
are going to
get me in trouble.

yea
i oughta

duct-tape my pecker
to my asshole,
he says.

speak of the devil,
i say
as a pack of them
come jogging by:
it's the cross country team
decked out
in school colors.

he's got
a bicycle horn
bolted
to the frame.

god bless america,
he says

honking it over
and over.

closest the old man and i ever got

after thanksgiving dinner
my dad, uncle allen and i
cruised gravel roads outside memphis missouri.
we stopped on a bridge over a frozen creek.
dad said the land used to be mankopf's farm,
how he and uncle allen would catch carp out of the creek
with their bare hands
and trade them with mr's mankopf for saltwater taffy.
uncle allen tossed his beer can down onto the ice
and went back to the car for another.
dad took a hit on his flask,
then he got the .44 out of the trunk.
he made the beer can jump straight into the air
three times with three shots.
he let me have a turn,
i missed badly.
then dad stood behind me,
cupping his hands over mine.
we pulled the trigger slowly
       making it turn somersaults
until the clip was empty.

full circle

my grandfather
showing me
how to work the
lever action rifle
out at
shimek woods.

holding a flashlight
for dad
while he
turned a wrench
to empty
the oil pan.

something steady
protective
about those arms.

today
squatting low
on the bank of the iowa river
teaching my little boy
how to properly
put a worm
on a hook.

he

leaning
in close
against me.

sixty-three years ago today

my father
was born
on a dirt floor
in hitt missouri

son of
hired help
on a chicken farm.

joseph william hyde

'buck' as he's known
to everyone
in the pool-hall.

joseph william hyde
drinking crown royal
in a crumbling
home in iowa he
never wanted
with a burned out
pill freak
for a wife

probably
on the couch
watching
black and white reruns
of cops
to mark the occasion.

i say probably
because i don't know

part of me cares to
if you can follow that.

joseph william hyde

fifty years
behind the world

five hundred miles away
from that dirt floor
in his hometown
which no longer
exists.

we've never
talked about it
never will
but someday
i'll be out there

waist deep in
prairie grass

his ashes
in my fist.

the last time i saw my father's dad

a line of drool
hung off
his chin–

the gravel road
vibrated it
onto his shirt.

help him
get that,
dad called
from the driver's
seat.

i scooted towards him
grabbed the handkerchief
from his overalls.

he was leaning
against the passenger door
and didn't move
while i
did it.

i was twelve

grandpa
had never put
more than five words
towards me.

in his day
he'd been a trick shot
sponsored by
a rifle manufacturer

but all i knew of him
was slumped in a chair

in the rotting apartment
above gerth
hardware.

we stopped
at a
rusty gate.

the three of us
stood
in front of
grandma's
grave.

grandpa said something

it was drowned out
by cicadas.

wind
blew the drool
across
his cheek.

i grabbed
the handkerchief
without being
asked.

getting your stripes

three handfuls of paunch
you've been fired from a job
lived with women
married to women
you no longer suck in that gut
when they come around;
another man's fists have beaten you down in the snow
you've beaten down another man in front of a flagpole
you avoid that game;
you've buried a loved one
cut the umbilical chord of your first born child
you've seen the sun go up
the sun go down
you hope for neither;
smirk of cholera
grace of bow-legged sage
you walk through strip-clubs
and sixteen car pileups
equally.

my mother never wore perfume

she didn't
use makeup either

or do much of anything
besides sleep.

the cheap perfumes
she'd accumulated
over decades of drunken
christmases and birthdays
at the hands of my father
were kept
in a cardboard box
under the stairs.

i don't know
why i started
pouring them
on the plywood-top
of the basement workbench
and lighting matches.

i wasn't trying to burn the house down.

i wasn't hoping to get caught for attention.

i wasn't sexually excited.

i've decided
that drowning silence
as the flames licked my wrist
was a level of nirvana
such to make buddha himself
jealous.

practicing

he has beautiful
blue eyes,
says the old man
in brown suspenders
walking through the mall
with a
blind man's cane.

how old is
the boy?
he asks
smiling down at
my son.

two years
in august,
i say
trying not to stare into
those
cloudy eyes.

hell of a thing
being young,
he says
holding out the white cane
like a
dead cat.

hell of a thing,
i nod.

gonna hafta
get used to this,
he says
striking the dull metal tip
against the cold
tile floor.

girl on third shift at the kum and go

played billy graham sermons
on a cd
over the speaker system.

told me
she hadn't always done
the right thing

but she was enrolling at dmacc
gonna get her aa
maybe be a dental hygienist
or a court reporter.

i was in every morning
around five
power-bar and coffee
before my shift as a temp
at hach.

she always
tucked her hair
behind her ears
smiled
after ringing me up.

very little enamel on her teeth

amateur tattoo
of a spider
on the patch of skin
between her thumb
and forefinger.

you could tell
she hadn't always done
the right thing

but she had a kind face.

i was working up courage
to ask her out for dinner

snipped a rose
from my parent's neighbors
tied a little note to it

but she wasn't there
four days in a row.

finally asked the manager
filling in for her.

said he didn't know

she'd just stopped showing
and her phone
was disconnected.

taking inventory on a hundred boxes of rubber grommets

the other temp finally showed

two hours late:

sheila was three hundred pounds
lived in a HUD shit-box over in boone
with her mother
and four kids
from three different guys.

she chewed valium like tic-tacs

everyday was either empty mania
or some new phantasm
throwing her life into crisis.

hey there hot-pants,
was what she usually
said to me
first thing in the morning -

pinching my ass
if she caught me
from behind.

that day
she didn't say anything
just sat down
at the little table
behind the forklift.

got my head
out of that box of grommets
signed off on the clipboard
turned around to say hello
and noticed she was crying.

what's going on sheila?

i sat across from her
waiting to hear the latest
orange-juice tragedy.

she told me
her cat got run over
in the parking lot
last night.

she said
his little brains
were coming out of his head.

then she started wailing
and asked me to please
hold her.

which i did.

you think you've seen everything

silver-dollar eyed
guy in the corner
of the flying-j
talking gibberish
loudly
to himself.

that's nothing
we've all
seen it.

but still

after pissing
you ask the waitress
if he's alright.

he's a regular,
she says.
a Vietnam
vet.

that makes sense.
you go back to
reading a little
sartre.

he jumps out of his
booth.

starts doing the
twist.

6'3
250 pound
bear of a man

grinding it out

like a
motherfucker

smiling from
one end of the room
to the other

belting out chubby checker
so loud
it's vibrating your
ribcage
seven booths over.

he comes toward
your booth.

motions for you to
get up and dance.

it's not fear
and it's not
pity.

you don't
exactly know
what the hell
is going on.

but
you do it.

after falling through the camel's eye

you start to understand
grown men
tending gardens

&

human shapes
flinging themselves
off the top level
of parking ramps.

you empathize with
ufo conspiracists

overweight housewives
with a neurotic attachment
to coupons

&

the genius apathy
of water.

after falling through the camel's eye
an old laotian
in a five gallon hat
sitting next to you at south-port
on a monday morning says:

hey chum pal chum help me with this:

he pours a shot of 151
over his palm:

you don't hesitate
plucking
the black heads
of six roots

out of the wart
with a rusty tweezers
while he holds the
flesh open with his pocket knife
and simultaneously
tries selling you
three hundred dollars of counterfeit twenties
for thirty-five bucks:

or maybe straight up
for those fancy running shoes
you got there
make offer tom-dick-joe,
he smiles
through
no teeth.

it didn't work out

at the chuckie cheese
in saint louis
with my girlfriend
and her two
half-sisters.

the picture-booth
in the game-room
made an automated
sketch.

the four of us
crammed in there,
then sarah
stuck with it.

she popped more tokens
took her shoe off
and held it
up to the viewer.

she was in
third grade.

her father
had left them
and gone to florida
three months ago.

she grabbed a piece of pizza
off our table,
dropped more tokens
and held it up.

i handed her a five
and said
let's see if it can get
lincoln's beard.

it
did.

she wondered
if it would work
upside down.

i did
a handstand.

she smiled wide
as i'd seen
in my two days there.

are you
gonna marry my sister?
she asked
while grabbing my hand
and leading me
to the skee-ball lanes.

i hope so.

me too,
she said
and locked
a bear hug.

in the hospital cafeteria while my son has eye surgery

man
hips like a buffalo
bright blue suspenders
stood in front of the garbage can
for an inordinate amount of time.

damndest thing
the garbage talks to you,
he finally turned away
and said to me.

and it did.

thank you for putting your trash
in the receptacle,
came a female voice
with a british accent
out of a speaker built into it.

walking out
i passed by the man in blue suspenders:

he was standing behind a strange wheelchair
it had three large wheels
and was tilted back at an angle.

in it
was an emaciated old man
green tinted skin
his eyes were closed.

standing at the elevator
waiting to go down to my son's floor
they came up behind me.

almost done for the day dad
one more round

and we can go home,
said the man in suspenders.

the old man didn't respond
he just laid there
eyes still closed.

the doors opened.

i asked the man in suspenders
what floor they needed.

third floor
chemo,
he said.

the silver doors closed.

it lurched slightly
as we started to move.

the old man opened his eyes
they were black
vivid as shoe polish.

i nodded to him
without an ounce of pity.

he nodded back
like people used to
when looking a man in the eyes
meant something.

they don't make them
like that
anymore.

at the harvest cafe

the twenty year old woman
sitting across from me
is stacking
our plates and silverware.

she does this
every restaurant we go to

she used to be a waitress
knows how hard they work.

i wipe syrup
off my fork
ask her
what she wants to do
after we go
to iowa city.

i don't want
to go,
she says
biting her lower lip
disappearing
somewhere in her
mind.

she's very tired
this morning
bags under her eyes

but you'd never guess
she's full of
cancer.

only me
and a couple of her
close friends at college
know.

won't tell her family

doesn't want them
to worry.

let's run away
to jamaica
right now,
she says.

anything you want
honey,
i say
holding her hand
under the table.

little church in the basement of the county hospital

the book
was at the back
on a lectern
next to a cup of
pencils.

i opened
it.

people had written
pleas
to the almighty
for uncles, grandfathers
and mothers.

better off
robbing a bank
and flying in
some specialists,
i thought

but still
wrote:

please save my
girlfriend
dying of cancer
in room 314.

people across the street lost a son in iraq

i notice
a basketball hoop
over the garage

a lamp turned on
in their
living room

i go check
on my six month old
son

gently
put my hand
on his stomach

we move slowly
up and down

knives
at the stone.

the closest i've come to making love

at the very end
it spread into her spine
her back was so
shot she didn't get out of bed
to use the
restroom.

i'd slide a pillow underneath
her and hold
an ice pack
to her forehead.

just talk,
she said.

don't stop
talking.

the man watching harness racing at the bar

we get to
talking sports:

an iowa state fan
he says the last football coach
got fired
because he played too conservative with a lead.

says
when he was a kid
his father
taught him two things:

don't let someone else
tell you how to feel
and
if you get in a fight
never take your foot off their throat
until the job's done.

he keeps
motioning me
to talk into his right ear.

i ask
what happened to the left.

he pulls off
a worn
brown leather belt
with a dull silver buckle
and lays it out
flat on the bar.

my old man
heeded his own philosophy,
he says.

tells me
between the ages of
four and sixteen
he probably got it
to the side of the head
a couple hundred times.

go ahead,
he says

feel it in your hands.

dennis 36 years

first thing i noticed
about the man
who came to fix my
garbage disposal
was his name tag:

dennis
36 years.

without saying a word
he made his way to my kitchen

white five gallon bucket
in his left hand
serving as a tool-box.

he pulled an old blanket
out of the bucket

spread it on the floor
beneath the sink
and crouched down.

i'm fascinated
and appalled
by the kind of people
who work 36 years
at the same job.

personally
i've never lasted
more than a year and a half
at any turn.

sitting on the edge of the bed
in my efficiency apt
i pretended to read

a book of short stories
by chekhov

but i watched him work

wanting to know
what kind of thoughts
ran through his mind
on a daily basis

like sherwood anderson
i'm intrigued by the
grotesques

but if you pay
any kind of attention in this life
you know you don't
ask those kinds of questions outright
to the type of people
who work 36 years
at the same job.

i heard his wrench
drop to the floor.
bat-full of hell,
he said
and kept working.

a few minutes later
he put the towel
in the bucket
and stood up.

she'll take the full load,
he said
and walked past me
and let himself out.

that night

i was sideways
on crown and seven

playing the clown
for my first
fuck-buddy in ten years

and i stubbed my little toe
on her bedpost.

bat-full of hell,
i said
limping it off.

what'd you just say?
she called from the bed
where she sat cross-legged
in pigtails
painting her
fingernails black.

bat-full of hell
it's not my line
i stole it
from dennis 36 years,
i said
looking down there
to make sure
i hadn't sheared off
the toe.

wha?

never mind,
i said
and got up there properly
and set the polish on the bed-stand
before giving her
the full load.

i've lost the thread

says whetstone
rubbing the front
of his bald head
with the palm
of his right hand.

he's in work release
for stalking:
got caught
up in a tree
masturbating
while videotaping
a woman
undressing.

he's spent
the last three hours
up at the control desk
telling me how
the jehovahs brainwashed him:
but he finally caught on
they were selling jesus short
he stole a motorcycle
ended up at a psych ward
in washington state
where a nurse told him something
that's stuck in his mind
like a hatchet
in a stump.

that's the ticket,
he says
and slaps his forehead
and tells me:

religion
is for those who fear hell.

spirituality is for those
who've been there.

at the time
he thought it was
just a catchy
aphorism.

but that was before
he married that navajo stripper
down in
fort lauderdale.

arms length

at arms length
we can be
best friends

or even
lovers.

any
closer

i'm something
like
an arsonist.

this garden, carefully tended, for 32years

the music
is old

the colors
are stale

the air
is feeble

your own voice
and the
insipid gears
behind it
bore you.

entirely
rootless

save for
one night stands
out of the waveland

and this
three year old boy
driving a
red remote control truck
up and down
your living room floor

to whom what
you wonder

if anything

you have to offer.

no solidarity

there's no solidarity anymore,
says the white haired trucker
with peach colored skin
one booth ahead of me at the flying j.
i'd just asked him
about the possibility of a trucker's strike
over gas prices
like they had in china.
every man for hiself nowadays
lucky for me i'm on the way out, he says.
gonna get a whole lot worse
before it gets better, says his wife
staring through both of us
with the fierce intelligent eyes
of a hawk.
men talking here evelyn, he says
cutting them down
into her lap.

she told me her mother slept with a snub-nosed revolver

the bow-walled trailer
was in a bad neighborhood
outside of saint louis.

my girlfriend
and her mom
went to take cans back
and get some hotdogs
for dinner.

i played a nascar game
on the x-box
with her boyfriend.

rodney told me
the bricklayer's union
had been thin
but it'd pick up
in a month or two.
he had big plans
to build a deck
out front.

it was known
that he beat
her mother.

at the time
there was a bruise
taking color
across her left
cheek.

the sleeves
of his flannel shirt
were rolled up

he had the forearms

of a body builder

L O V E
was tattooed
on the four fingers
of his right hand.

their toilet
was busted.

when he went
to the neighbors
to take a shit
i walked back
into their bedroom.

it was there
under the
pillow.

i swung out
the cylinder.

the chambers
were full.

a garbage bag
was taped
over a cracked
window.

the headboard
was covered
in small pewter
unicorns.

whaddya doin'
in mom's room?

her four year old
half-sister
who had been sleeping
was standing
in the doorway.

i wanted to see
the unicorns,
i said
while sliding the revolver
tight down my thigh
and back
under the pillow.

this is her favorite,
she grabbed one
and held it out
in her palm.

there was
a deep groove
worn
into its side.

she showed me
how her mother
rubbed it
back and forth
with her thumb
for good luck.

Also by Justin Hyde

DOWN WHERE THE HUMMINGBIRD GOES TO DIE
Tainted Coffee Press (2008)

ANOTHER CASUALTY AT THE 34TH STREET BUS STOP
Nerve Cowboy (2009)

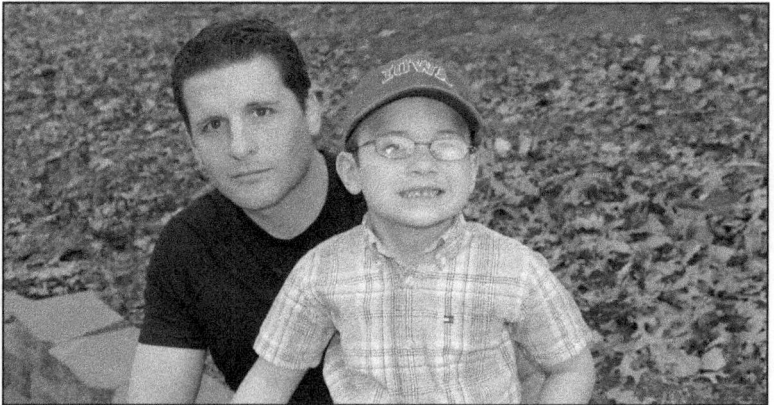

Justin Hyde currenly lives in Iowa, USA.

The author gratefully acknowledges the following publications who have supported his work, and where many of these poems first appeared.

The Iowa Review	Fox Chase Review
The New York Quarterly	Elimae
FriGG Magazine	Catch-Up
Word Riot	Clutching at Straws
Poiesis Review	Orion Headless
Counterpunch	Flutter
Pigpen	The Bicycle Review
Poetry Super Highway	Fuck!
Orange Room Review	Yes
Black Listed	Poetry Cemetery
Milk	Leaf Garden Press
Unlikely Stories	Poetry Midwest
Chronogram	Opium Poetry
Beat the Dust	Winamop
Gutter Eloquence	deComp
Boy Slut	13miles from Cleveland
Mad Swirl	The Smoking Poet
3am	Coe Review
Nibble	Gloom Cupboard
Common-line	Cherry Bleeds
Red fez	Dead Snakes
Strange Road	Fight These Bastards
Rusty Truck	The Camel Saloon
Clockwise Cat	Concrete Meat Sheet
Asphodel Madness	Camroc Press
Ink Sweat and Tears	Amarillo Bay
Underground Voices	Denver Syntax
Lit Up Magazine	Haggard & Halloo
My Favorite Bullet	The Panulaan Review
Horror Sleaze Trash	Weird Year
Thieves Jargon	Little White Poetry Journal
Carcinogenic Poetry	Ygdrasil
Laura Hird	Mississippi Crow
Zygote In My Coffee	Slice

ip

www.interiornoisepress.com

www.ingramcontent.com/pod-product-compliance
Lightning Source LLC
Chambersburg PA
CBHW022008100426
42736CB00041B/1019